Dean Burgon Society Deserves Its Name
TEN REASONS WHY

Dean John William Burgon
(1813-1888)

Pastor D. A. Waite, Th.D., Ph.D.
President, The Dean Burgon Society

Published by

**The Dean Burgon Society Press
Box 354
Collingswood, New Jersey 08108
U.S.A.**

March, 2001

#1847

Copyright, 2001
All Rights Reserved

ISBN #1-888328-08-8

DEDICATION

- To the many Dean Burgon members, some of whom have been a part of the Dean Burgon Society since its beginning in November, 1978.

- To the DBS Executive Committee members and the DBS Advisory Council members who have helped in speaking, recruiting, writing, and giving to this cause.

- And to the many, who, though they are not DBS members, share in our position **"IN DEFENSE OF TRADITIONAL BIBLE TEXTS."**

ACKNOWLEDGMENTS

This is to acknowledge the valuable assistance of Yvonne Sanborn Waite, Daniel Waite, and Miss Barbara Egan for their careful proofreading of the manuscript and helpful suggestions.

FOREWORD

- This book began as a message that was first given at the Calvary Baptist Church, in Warren, Maine, when Dr. Don Champeon was the Pastor. The occasion was the 12th Annual Dean Burgon Society Conference. The date was Thursday, May 31, 1990. It is available, as delivered, either in audio cassette (#1850/5 for a gift of $4.00+S&H) or in video cassette (#1850/VC2 for a gift of $15.00+S&H). The message has been available as a 67-page report since that time. This book is the result of scanning that report of the 1990 message and putting it into the present format with a few additions, subtractions, and changes as needed.
- The present edition gives ten sound reasons why our Dean Burgon Society deserves its name. These reasons are formed by an acrostic of the ten letters of Dean Burgon's name. The reasons are just as true today, in the year 2001, as they were in 1990. As Dean Burgon, the Dean Burgon Society is (1) defending, (2) educational, (3) adamant, (4) neglected, (5) believing, (6) undaunted, (7) relevant, (8) growing, (9) obedient, and (10) needed.
- For many years now, almost from its very beginning in 1978, the Dean Burgon Society has been vilified, misunderstood, criticized, and even slandered for taking to itself the honored name of Dean John William Burgon (1813-1888). I believe the reason for these attacks stems from ignorance--ignorance either of the position of Dean Burgon or of the Dean Burgon Society, or both. It is hoped that this book will help to dispel such ignorance. It is also hoped that all who read it will agree with these ten reasons which show that the Dean Burgon Society truly deserves its name!

D. a. Waite
Pastor D. A. Waite, Th.D., Ph.D.
President, The Dean Burgon Society
March 15, 2001

> Proverbs 22:1
> "**A good name** is rather to be chosen than great riches, . . ."
> Ecclesiastes 7:1
> **A good name** is better than precious ointment; . . ."

TABLE OF CONTENTS

SECTION   **PAGE**

Dedication iii
Acknowledgments iv
Foreword v
Table of Contents vii
INTRODUCTORY REMARKS 1
    A.   The History Of Our Name 1
    B.   Two Areas Of Difference 1
         1.   Specific Work And Ministry 1
         2.   Doctrinal Basis 1
    C.   An Acrostic 2

CHAPTER I
AS DEAN BURGON, THE DEAN BURGON SOCIETY
IS A DEFENDING SOCIETY 3
    A.   **Dean Burgon Was A DEFENDING Individual** 3
         1.   Burgon **DEFENDED** The Old Testament Masoretic Hebrew Text 3
             a.   Burgon Thought "Tinkering the Hebrew Text" Was "Incredible Folly" 3
             b.   Burgon Took The Old Testament "Simply on The Authority of The Divine Master" 3
         2.   Burgon **DEFENDED** The New Testament Textus Receptus Greek Text 3
             a.   Summary Of Dean Burgon's Views On The Textus Receptus 3
             b.   Examples Of Dean Burgon's Views On The Textus Receptus 3
                (1)   Burgon Esteemed the "Received Text" To Be "Quite Good Enough For All Ordinary Purposes" 4
                (2)   Burgon Believed The Textus Receptus to Be "An Excellent Text as it Stands,"And That The Use of it Will Never Lead Critical Students of Scripture Seriously Astray" 4
                (3)   Burgon Estimated The Textus Receptus To Be The True Text "In Nine Cases Out of Ten" 4
                (4)   Burgon Listed Fourteen Requirements For Any Revision of The Textus Receptus Proving Why In His Day Such a Revision Was Impossible 4

- (5) Burgon Believed That For An "Authoritative Revision of The Greek Text" They Were "Not Yet Mature" In His Day 5
- (6) Burgon Demanded At Least Six Prerequisites Before Any Authoritative Revision of The Textus Receptus Could Be Successfully Completed ... 6
  - (a) Prerequisite #1: We Need at Least "500 More Copies" of The New Testament "Diligently Collated" 6
  - (b) Prerequisite #2: We Need at Least "100" "Ancient Lectionaries" "Very Exactly Collated" 6
  - (c) Prerequisite #3: We Need, "Above All," The Church "Fathers" to Yield "Their Precious Secrets" by "Ransacking" Them, "Indexing" Them, And "Diligently Inspecting" Them 7
  - (d) Prerequisite #4: We Need the "Most Important of The Ancient Versions" to Be "Edited Afresh" And Let Their "Languages" Be "Really Mastered by Englishmen" 7
  - (e) Prerequisite #5: We Need "Whatever Unpublished Works of The Ancient Greek Fathers" to Be "Printed" 7
  - (f) Prerequisite #6: We Need "For The First Time" The "Science of Textual Criticism" to Be Prosecuted "In a Scholarlike Manner" 7
- c. Proof That Neither The "Nestle-Aland Greek Text--26th or 27th Edition" Nor The So-called "Majority Greek Text of Hodges & Farstad" Followed Burgon's Six Prerequisites And Are Therefore Not What Burgon Would Call "Authoritative Revisions" of The Textus Receptus 7
  - (1) The "Nestle-Aland Greek Text--26th or 27th Edition" Refused to Follow Burgon's Six Prerequisites and Therefore Is Not What Burgon Would Call an "Authoritative Revision" of the Textus Receptus 8
  - (2) The So-called "Majority Greek Text" of Hodges & Farstad Also Refused to Follow Burgon's Six Prerequisites and Therefore Is NOT What Burgon Would Call An "Authoritative Revision" of The Textus Receptus 9
3. Burgon **DEFENDED** The King James Bible 10

Table of Contents ix

    a. Burgon Believed The "Men of 1611" Produced "A Work of Real Genius" 10
    b. Burgon Stated That The King James Bible Translators "Understood Their Craft" and That "The Spirit of Their God, Was Mightily upon Them" 10
    c. Burgon Considered the King James Bible to Be "The Noblest Literary Work in the Anglo-Saxon Language" 10
    d. Burgon Would Not "Entertain for a Moment" The Project of Any "Rival Translation" to the King James Bible 11
    e. Burgon Thought Any Revision of the King James Bible Should Be in a Way like "Marginal Notes" or a Similar Way 11
    f. Burgon Thought of Any Revision of the King James Bible as Only a "Companion in the Study" for "Private Edification" 11
    g. Burgon Was Against Any "Future Revision" of the English New Testament until an "Authoritative Revision of the Greek Text" Had Been Completed 11

4. Burgon **DEFENDED** the Plenary, Verbal Inspiration and Inerrancy of the Sixty-six Books of the Bible 11
    a. Burgon Held That the Very "Words" of the Bible Were "Inspired," and "Every Syllable" as Well 12
    b. Burgon Also Believed in Plenary, Verbal Inspiration of "Every Book" of the Bible 12
    c. Burgon Denied Any "Inspiration" of Any Kind to the "Apocryphal Books" 12
    d. Burgon Believed That Verbal Inspiration of the Bible Extended down to the "Very Letters" 12
    e. Burgon Repeated His Firm Belief in the Verbal "Inspiration" of "Every 'Jot' and Every 'Tittle'" of the Bible 12
    f. Burgon Also Believed in the Inerrancy of The Bible Since "No Error or Blot of Any Kind" Could "Possibly Exist Within its Pages" 13
    g. Burgon Believed That When You "Read the Bible" You must Believe "That You Are Reading an Inspired Book" Which Is "Inspired in Every Part" 13
    h. Burgon Did Not Believe Preachers Could "Expound a Text" Unless They Believed "The Words" to Be "Inspired" 13

5. Burgon **DEFENDED** Against Heresy in His Anglican Church 13

a. Burgon Was a "Watch-dog" Who "Barked Furiously" When Even "The Smallest Danger Threatened the Church or the Faith" 13
b. Burgon "Hit His Opponents Rather Hard" Because the "Words of Inspiration" Were "Seriously Imperilled" 14
c. Burgon Thwarted the "Liberal Party" at Oxford University on "More than One Occasion" by His "unflinching Conservatism" 14
d. Burgon Preached a Sermon Against the "Disestablishment of Religion in Oxford" Which Was Removing Belief in the "Thirty-nine Articles of Faith" 14
e. Burgon Wrote a Lengthy Criticism of *"Essays and Reviews"* Six of Whose Authors Were "Ministers of the Church of England" Who Were "Making Light of Their Sacred Profession" 15
f. Burgon Agreed with an Infidel's Description of the Apostasy Contained in the *"Essays and Reviews"* Which He Refuted 15
g. Burgon "Handled" the Writers of *"Essays and Reviews"* Just as "Freely" as They Handled "Divine Truth" .. 15
h. Burgon Identified the Authors of *"Essays and Reviews"* as Being Guilty of "Blasphemy," "Irreligion," and "Infidelity" 16
i. Burgon Believed *"Essays and Reviews"* Sapped the "Foundation of Faith" 16
j. Burgon Did Not Think "Punctilious Courtesy" Should Be Practiced in Denouncing Those Who Handle the Things of God in an "Outrageous Manner" 16
k. Burgon Exposed His Church's Clergymen Who Denied the "Fact of Our Lord's Resurrection" as "The Worst Enemies of Christ" 16
l. Burgon Urged His Fellow Anglican Clergymen Who Were Heretics to "Recall Their Words" or "Resign Their Stations" 17

6. Burgon **DEFENDED** Against the Heresy of Romanism and "Romanizing Practices" Within His Church 17
   a. Burgon "Abhorred" "Romanism" 17
   b. Burgon "Condemned Entirely" the Roman Catholic Error of "Prayer for the Dead" 17
   c. Burgon Was Opposed to Either "Ritualism" or "Romanizing Practices" in His Church 17
   d. Burgon Protested Strongly Against a "Florid Ritual"

Table of Contents

Which Made "Communion" Similar to the "Roman Mass" 18
e. Burgon Opposed "Romanising and Ritualising Tendencies" in His Church as Well as "Rationalism" Which Was "Undermining The Faith" 18
f. Burgon Was So Much Against "Romanizing" of His Church That He Preached Two Sermons Against it in 1873 18
g. Burgon Repudiated the Two Resolutions Made by the Oxford Diocesan Conference Which Furthered the "Romanising Movement Within the Church of England" 18
h. Burgon Preached Against the "Ritualists" and Various "Romish Doctrines" Which He Called "Mediaevalism in the Church of England" 19
7. Burgon **Defended** Against the Errors of the English Revised Version of 1881 and the Underlying Greek Text 19
   a. Burgon Believed the ERV's "Revision of the Sacred Text" Was "Untrustworthy from Beginning to End" 19
   b. Burgon Felt He Had "Crushed the Revised Version" of 1881 So it Would "Never Lift up its Head Again" .. 20

B. As DEAN BURGON, The DEAN BURGON SOCIETY Is A DEFENDING Society 20
1. The DBS Motto Is "in **DEFENSE** of Traditional Bible Texts" 20
2. As Dean Burgon, the DBS **DEFENDS** the "Masoretic Hebrew Text" 20
3. As Dean Burgon, the DBS **DEFENDS** The "Textus Receptus" 20
4. As Dean Burgon, The DBS **DEFENDS** the King James Bible 20
5. As Dean Burgon, The DBS **DEFENDS** the Plenary, Verbal Inspiration and Inerrancy Of All Sixty-Six Books Of The Bible 21
6. As Dean Burgon, The DBS **DEFENDS** Against the Heresy of Romanism 21
7. As Dean Burgon, The DBS **DEFENDS** Against Westcott and Hort's Greek Text 21
8. As Dean Burgon, the DBS **DEFENDS** Against the English Revised Version of 1881 22

CHAPTER II
AS DEAN BURGON, THE DEAN BURGON SOCIETY IS AN EDUCATIONAL SOCIETY 23

A. Dean Burgon Was An EDUCATIONAL Individual 23
   1. Burgon **EDUCATED** By Writing His Many Books On The Traditional Text 23
   2. Burgon **EDUCATED** By Training Men For The Ministry 23

B. As DEAN BURGON, The DEAN BURGON SOCIETY Is An EDUCATIONAL Society 23
   1. The Dean Burgon Society **EDUCATES** By Its *DBS News* 23
   2. The Dean Burgon Society **EDUCATES** By Its Printed Pamphlets 23
   3. The Dean Burgon Society **EDUCATES** By Its Annual Meetings On Audio and Video Cassettes 24
   4. The Dean Burgon Society **EDUCATES** By Its *"Articles of Faith"* 24
   5. The Dean Burgon Society **EDUCATES** By Making Over 1,000 Titles Available In Defense Of the King James Bible And Its Underlying Texts 24

CHAPTER III
AS DEAN BURGON, THE DEAN BURGON SOCIETY IS AN ADAMANT SOCIETY 25

A. Dean Burgon Was An ADAMANT Individual ... 25
   1. Burgon Was **ADAMANT** In His Refusal to Compromise In General 25
      a. Burgon **Refused** to Compromise In General by Sticking to His Colours 25
      b. Burgon **Refused** to Compromise In General by Delivering Himself with Courage 25
      c. Burgon **Refused** to Compromise In General by His "Indomitable Force of Will" 25
      d. Burgon **Refused** to Compromise In General by His Obvious "Sincerity" 25
   2. Burgon Was **ADAMANT** In His Refusal to Compromise On The Word Of God 26
      a. Burgon **Refused** To Compromise On The Word Of

		God By "Maintaining the Integrity of the Written Word of God" 26

      b.   Burgon **Refused** To Compromise On The Word Of God By His "Burning Zeal" For It 26

      c.   Burgon **Refused** To Compromise On The Word Of God By Maintaining "A Burning Zeal for the Word of God" as a "Champion in a Cause" 26

      d.   Burgon **Refused** To Compromise on the Word of God by His "Reverence" For It 26

      e.   Burgon **Refused** To Compromise on the Word of God by "Treasuring" it as "Infinitely Precious" 26

B. **As DEAN BURGON, The DEAN BURGON SOCIETY Is An ADAMANT Society** 26

   1.   As Dean Burgon, The DBS Is **ADAMANT** In Its Refusal To Compromise In General 26

   2.   As Dean Burgon, The DBS Is **ADAMANT** In Its Stand On the Texts and Translations Of The Bible 27

CHAPTER IV
AS DEAN BURGON, THE DEAN BURGON SOCIETY IS A NEGLECTED SOCIETY 30

A. **Dean Burgon Was A NEGLECTED Individual** ... 30

   1.   Burgon Was **NEGLECTED** By Not Being On The English Revised Version (ERV) Of 1881 30

   2.   Burgon Was **NEGLECTED** By His Being Attacked Or Laughed At 30

   3.   Burgon Was **NEGLECTED** By NOT Being Elevated To Anglican Bishop, Only To Dean 30

B. **As DEAN BURGON, The DEAN BURGON SOCIETY Is A NEGLECTED Society** 30

   1.   As Dean Burgon, The DBS Is **NEGLECTED** By Being Little Known 30

   2.   As Dean Burgon, The DBS Is **NEGLECTED** By Being Attacked, Set Aside, and Laughed at 31

CHAPTER V
AS DEAN BURGON, THE DEAN BURGON SOCIETY IS A BELIEVING SOCIETY 32

A. **Dean Burgon Was A BELIEVING Individual** 32

   1.   Burgon Was A **BELIEVING** Individual By Holding To The

Plenary, Verbal Inspiration Of The Bible 32
2. Burgon Was A **BELIEVING** Individual By Urging The Reading Of The Bible From Genesis To Revelation 32
3. Burgon Was a **BELIEVING** Individual By Holding To The Creation Of The World In Six Literal Days 32
4. Burgon Was A **BELIEVING** Individual By Trusting In The "Blood" Of Christ For Salvation 33

B. As DEAN BURGON, The DEAN BURGON SOCIETY Is A BELIEVING Society 33
1. As Dean Burgon, The DBS Is **BELIEVING** In The Plenary, Verbal Inspiration Of The Bible 33
2. As Dean Burgon, The DBS Is **BELIEVING** In The Reading Of And The Power Of The Bible 33
3. As Dean Burgon, The DBS Is **BELIEVING** By Holding To The Creation Of The World In Six Literal Days 33
4. As Dean Burgon, The DBS Is **BELIEVING** In The "Blood" Of Christ To Save 34

CHAPTER VI
AS DEAN BURGON, THE DEAN BURGON SOCIETY IS AN UNDAUNTED SOCIETY 35

A. Dean Burgon Was An UNDAUNTED Individual . 35
1. Burgon Was **UNDAUNTED** In His Efforts To Defeat The "English Revised Version" 35
2. Burgon Was **UNDAUNTED** In His Efforts To Defeat Westcott And Hort's Greek Text 35
3. Burgon Was **UNDAUNTED** In His Efforts To Defend The Very Words Of God 35
4. Burgon Was **UNDAUNTED** In His Efforts In Study And Written Ministry 36
5. Burgon Was **UNDAUNTED** In The Face Of Criticism And Misunderstanding 36

B. As DEAN BURGON, The DEAN BURGON SOCIETY Is An UNDAUNTED Society 36
1. As Dean Burgon, The DBS Is **UNDAUNTED** In Its Efforts To Defeat The English Revised Version And Similar False Versions 37
2. As Dean Burgon, The DBS Is **UNDAUNTED** In Its Efforts To Defeat Westcott And Hort's Greek Text 37

3. As Dean Burgon, The DBS Is **UNDAUNTED** In Its Efforts To Defend The Very Words Of God 37
   4. As Dean Burgon, The DBS Is **UNDAUNTED** In Its Efforts To Study And Maintain A Written Ministry 37
   5. As Dean Burgon, The DBS Is **UNDAUNTED** In Its Efforts In The Face of Criticism And Misunderstanding 38

CHAPTER VII
AS DEAN BURGON, THE DEAN BURGON SOCIETY IS A RELEVANT SOCIETY 39

A. **Dean Burgon Was RELEVANT As An Individual** 39
   1. Burgon Was **RELEVANT** In Defending Bible Truth Against Error And Heresy 39
   2. Burgon Was **RELEVANT** In Defending The King James Bible Against An Inferior Version 39
   3. Burgon Was **RELEVANT** In Defending The Masoretic Hebrew Text That Underlies The King James Bible 39
   4. Burgon Was **RELEVANT** In Defending The Traditional & Received Greek Text 39

B. **As DEAN BURGON, The DEAN BURGON SOCIETY Is A RELEVANT Society** 39
   1. As Dean Burgon, The DBS Is **RELEVANT** In Defending Bible Truth Against Error And Heresy 40
   2. As Dean Burgon, The DBS Is **RELEVANT** In Defending The King James Bible Against Inferior Versions 40
   3. As Dean Burgon, The DBS Is **RELEVANT** In Defending The Masoretic Hebrew Text 40
   4. As Dean Burgon, The DBS Is **RELEVANT** In Defending The Traditional And Received Greek Text 40

CHAPTER VIII
AS DEAN BURGON, THE DEAN BURGON SOCIETY IS A GROWING SOCIETY 42

A. **Dean Burgon Was A GROWING Individual** 42
   1. Burgon Was **GROWING** In The Knowledge Of The Scripture 42
   2. Burgon Was **GROWING** In The Understanding Of The Scripture 42
   3. Burgon Was **GROWING** In Encouraging Others To Follow Him In His Use Of Scripture 42

- B. **As DEAN BURGON, The DEAN BURGON SOCIETY Is A GROWING Society** 43
  1. As Dean Burgon, The DBS Is **GROWING** In The Knowledge Of The Scripture 43
  2. As Dean Burgon, The DBS Is **GROWING** In The Understanding Of The Scripture 43
  3. As Dean Burgon, The DBS Is **GROWING** In Their Encouraging Of Others To Follow Their Position 43

CHAPTER IX
AS DEAN BURGON, THE DEAN BURGON SOCIETY IS AN OBEDIENT SOCIETY 44

- A. **Dean Burgon Was An OBEDIENT Individual** 44
  1. Burgon Was **OBEDIENT** In Exposing Error 44
     a. Burgon Was Like A "Splendid Watch Dog" 44
     b. Burgon Admitted He Defended Strenuously When the "Words of Inspiration Are Seriously Imperilled" .. 44
     c. Burgon "Thwarted," by His "Conservatism," the "Liberal Party" at Oxford More than Once 44
     d. Burgon Labeled "Disbelief in the Bible as the Word of God" as the "Fundamental Error" 45
     e. Burgon Wanted to "Defend" the Bible "Without Compromise" 45
     f. Burgon Was "Jealous" For the "Honour of the Lord" 45
     g. Burgon Exposed the Heresies of "Six Ministers of the Church of England" in Their *"Essays and Reviews"* 45
        (1) The *"Essays and Reviews"* Denied the Fundamentals of the Faith 45
        (2) Burgon Treated the "Six Clergymen" as "Immoral Characters" 45
        (3) Burgon Did not Expect "Blasphemy" from "Ministers of the Gospel" 46
        (4) Burgon Denounced "Uncompromisingly" this "Volume" Which Was to "Sap The Foundation of Faith" 46
        (5) Burgon Gave an Example of Their Method of Believing Doctrine "Only Ideologically True" Yet "Historically False" 46
        (6) Burgon Held up to "Ridicule" and "Unqualified Reprobation" Those Ministers Who Put Forth Such "Blasphemous Folly" 47

(7) Burgon Called on the Heretical "Essayists and Reviewers" to "Resign Their Stations" in the Church 47
2. Burgon Was **OBEDIENT** In Defending The Bible 47
   a. Burgon Thought You Should Believe "The Whole of Holy Scripture" or "Disbelieve the Whole" 47
   b. Burgon Had Some Suggestions for Bible Reading and Bible Study for His Students Entering the Ministry . 48
     (1) the Bible Should Be His Students' Only Textbook for Three Years 48
     (2) His Students Should Read the "Whole Bible Consecutively Through" 48
     (3) His Students Should Spend the "Quietest Half-hour in the Whole Day" for Bible Reading 48
     (4) Bible Reading Should Be "Strictly Consecutive" 48
     (5) No Book or Chapter Should Be "Skipped" ... 48
   c. Burgon Gave Repeated Testimony to His Belief in and Defense of the Bible's Inspiration, Inerrancy, and Perfection 48
     (1) Burgon Believed the Bible Is a "Direct Message from the Presence-chamber of the Lord of Heaven and Earth" 49
     (2) Burgon Held "Verbal Inspiration" to Be a Fact, Not Merely a "Theory" 49
     (3) Burgon Believed Even the Very "Letters" of the Bible Were "Inspired" 50
     (4) Burgon Believed the Entire Bible to Be from God Himself and Vitally Important 50
       (a) Burgon Believed That Every "Word" Is Important 50
       (b) Burgon Believed Literally the Genesis Creation 50
       (c) Burgon Believed Every Single "Letter" of the Bible Is the "Voice of Him That Sitteth upon the Throne" 50
       (d) Burgon Repeated Again His Confidence in the Very "Words" of God as If "God Spoke to Us Therein with Human Lips" 50
       (e) Burgon Held the Bible to Be "The Very Utterance of the Holy Spirit" 51
       (f) Burgon Believed a Person Should "Read" the Bible Believing it Is an "Inspired Book" . 51

                (g) Burgon Didn't Believe You Could "Expound a Text" Unless You Believe its "Words" Are "Inspired" 51
                (h) Burgon Had a Burden and Passed it on to His Ministerial Students to "Preserve" the "Whole Deposit of the Heaven-descended Teaching" 52
                (i) Burgon Believed the Bible to Be a "Celestial Armoury" Which Contains a "Weapon" Against Every "Foe" 52
        3. Burgon Was **OBEDIENT** In Declaring Bible Truths .. 52
    B. **As DEAN BURGON, The DEAN BURGON SOCIETY Is An OBEDIENT Society** 53
        1. As Dean Burgon, The DBS Is **OBEDIENT** In Exposing Error And Heresy 53
        2. As Dean Burgon, The DBS Is **OBEDIENT** In Defending The Bible 53
        3. As Dean Burgon, The DBS Is **OBEDIENT** In Declaring Bible Truths 53

CHAPTER X
AS DEAN BURGON, THE DEAN BURGON SOCIETY IS A NEEDED SOCIETY 54

   A. **Dean Burgon Was A NEEDED Individual** 54
        1. Burgon Was **NEEDED** To Write Books And Materials 54
        2. Burgon Was **NEEDED** To Combat False Teaching 54
        3. Burgon Was **NEEDED** To Combat A False Basis Of Determining The Greek Text 54
        4. Burgon Was **NEEDED** To Get Out His Distinctive Message 54
   B. **As DEAN BURGON, The DEAN BURGON SOCIETY Is A NEEDED Society** 55
        1. As Dean Burgon, The DBS Is **NEEDED** To Write Books And Materials 55
        2. As Dean Burgon, The DBS Is **NEEDED** To Combat False Teaching 55
        3. As Dean Burgon, The DBS Is **NEEDED** To Combat A False Basis Of Determining The Greek Text 55
        4. As Dean Burgon, The DBS Is **NEEDED** To Get Out Our Distinctive Message 55

Table of Contents

CONCLUDING REMARKS 56
Index of Words and Phrases 57
About the Author 67
Order Blank #1 69
Order Blank #2 71
Order Blank #3 73
The *Defined King James Bibles* 75
Dean Burgon Society Membership Form 76

10 Reasons Why The Dean Burgon Society Deserves Its Name

By Pastor D. A. Waite, Th.D., Ph.D.
President, The Dean Burgon Society

Introductory Remarks

A. The History Of Our Name. The Dean Burgon Society, has borne its name since its founding, November 3-4, 1978, in Philadelphia, Pennsylvania. Over the course of years, some critics of our position have questioned the propriety of this designation. Though not seeking it, controversy dogged the steps of both Dean Burgon and the Dean Burgon Society. On the bottom of the first page of our *Dean Burgon News*, we print the following:

"The Dean Burgon Society, Inc. proudly takes its name in honor of Rev. John William Burgon (1813--1888), the Dean of Chichester in England, whose tireless and accurate scholarship and contribution in the area of New Testament Textual Criticism; whose defense of the Traditional Greek New Testament Text against its many enemies; and whose firm belief in the verbal inspiration and inerrancy of the Bible, we believe, have all been unsurpassed either before or since his time!"

B. Two Areas of Difference. It might be well at the outset to mention at least two areas in which the Dean Burgon Society differs from Dean Burgon.

1. Specific Work and Ministry. Our specific work and ministry is not identical to that of Dean Burgon. Our emphasis is outlined in our "Purpose and Object" found on pages 8-9 of our *"Articles of Faith, Operation, & Organization."* There are 13 specific objectives enumerated which guide the DBS in its work and ministry. Though we appreciate his guidelines on New Testament textual criticism and his excellent opposition to the Westcott and Hort-type Greek text, we as a Society have no intention of entering into the details of textual criticism as did Dean Burgon.

2. Doctrinal Basis. Our doctrinal basis is not identical to that of Dean Burgon. Our name does not imply we are Anglican in theology.

2   Ten Reasons Why DBS Deserves Its Name

Our "*Articles of Faith*" (pp. 2-6) spell out clearly our doctrinal position. In some areas, we are opposed to the tenets of the Church of England. One example of this would be in the area of "Salvation" (p. 5).

C. An Acrostic. I would suggest *"Ten Reasons Why the DBS Deserves its Name."* These ten reasons form an acrostic after the ten letters of the name, "D-E-A-N---B-U-R-G-O-N."

1. **"D"**--As Dean Burgon, The DBS is a **Defending** Society.
2. **"E"**--As Dean Burgon, The DBS is an **Educational** Society.
3. **"A"**--As Dean Burgon, The DBS is an **Adamant** Society.
4. **"N"**--As Dean Burgon, The DBS is a **Neglected** Society.

5. **"B"**--As Dean Burgon, The DBS is a **Believing** Society.
6. **"U"**--As Dean Burgon, The DBS is an **Undaunted** Society.
7. **"R"**--As Dean Burgon, The DBS is a **Relevant** Society.
8. **"G"**--As Dean Burgon, The DBS is a **Growing** Society.
9. **"O"**--As Dean Burgon, The DBS is an **Obedient** Society.
10. **"N"**--As Dean Burgon, The DBS is a **Needed** Society.

In the pages that follow, I would like to compare, in these ten respects, both Dean Burgon and the Dean Burgon Society. In some cases, I will give quotations fro m Dean Burgon's own words or the words of his biographer.

CHAPTER I
AS DEAN BURGON,
THE DEAN BURGON SOCIETY
IS A DEFENDING SOCIETY

A. Dean Burgon Was A DEFENDING Individual.
  1. Burgon DEFENDED the Old Testament Masoretic Hebrew Text.
   a. **Burgon Thought "Tinkering the Hebrew Text" Was "Incredible Folly."** Burgon wrote:
"Pray let us have the Revised Old Testament [of the E.R.V. of 1881] *by itself. It ought to contain a great deal well deserving of study, . . . above all if they have not been guilty of the "Incredible folly of tinkering the Hebrew Text."* [John William Burgon--Late Dean of Chichester--A Biography, Two Volumes, (Hereafter called *"Biography"* by Dr. Edward Meyrick Goulburn, Vol. II, p. 241; available as #1619, 801 pages, two volumes, for a GIFT of $40.00+S&H].
   b. **Burgon Took The Old Testament "Simply on the Authority of the Divine Master."** His biographer wrote:
"As to the authenticity of the supernatural narratives of the Old Testament, Burgon calls attention to the fact that the most marvellous of these, and those which have most proved stumbling-blocks, are witnessed to by our Lord and His Apostles; and that therefore we, as Christians, have no need to trouble ourselves with any independent consideration of the difficulties involved in them; we take them simply on the authority of the Divine Master, Who can neither deceive nor be deceived, and Who is sponsor for them." [Goulburn, *Biography*, Vol. II, p. 374]
  2. Burgon DEFENDED the New Testament Textus Receptus Greek Text.
First, let me give a brief summary of Burgon's views on the Textus Receptus, and then follow this with some examples of Burgon's views on the Textus Receptus.
   a. **Summary Of Dean Burgon's Views On The Textus Receptus.** It is important to see Dean Burgon's complete comments relative to the New Testament Textus Receptus Greek Text. Here are some of Dean Burgon's statements about the Textus Receptus.

4   Ten Reasons Why DBS Deserves Its Name

(1) The Textus Receptus as it now stands is "quite good enough for all ordinary purposes." It is *"an excellent text as it stands"* and the use of it *"will never lead critical students of the Scripture seriously astray."*

(2) The Textus Receptus is the "true" text in an estimated "nine cases out of ten [90%]." If Edward Miller's citation of Burgon's notes in his *Textual Commentary on Matthew 1-14*, [#1756 for a GIFT of $7.00+S&H] can be taken as a general trend, had Burgon completed his work, following his own guidelines, this 90% "true" figure for the Textus Receptus would have to be revised upward. The figure would be either 99.9% or 99.6% in favor of the Textus Receptus for Matthew 1-14, rather than merely an estimate of 90%! Here's how I arrive at these two figures:

(a) **The Textus Receptus 99.6% Accurate.** Though Edward Miller made many changes of his own, there were **only 39 changes** Miller made which were attributed to Dean Burgon's notes. There are 140,521 Greek words in the Textus Receptus Greek New Testament [Cf. *Missing in Modern Bibles* by Dr. Jack Moorman, p. 41; available as **#1726** for a GIFT of **$8.00**. There are 8,765 Greek words in the Textus Receptus for Matthew 1-14 [Cf. *Missing in Modern Bibles*, p. 38]. If **only 39 words** are changed, this is 39 out of 8,765 words, or only 0.4% changes. This means that there is **99.6% agreement** in Miller's work with the Textus Receptus where he quotes Dean Burgon. If this were the same percentage for the entire 140,521 Greek words in the Textus Receptus, it would only mean 0.4% x 140,521 or only a total of 562 words that would be changed in the New Testament. These **39 changes** break down as follows: Name spelling only = 5; change in word order only = 2; spelling only = 15; verb prefix only = 4; article only = 2; and **different words = 11**.

(b) **The Textus Receptus 99.9% Accurate.** If the **"different words"** are the only major changes to be noted, this would be **11 words** out of a possible 8,765 or only 0.12%. This means there is **99.9% agreement** in Miller's work with the Textus Receptus where he quotes Dean Burgon. If this were the same percentage for the entire 140,521 Greek words in the Textus Receptus, it would only mean 0.12% x 140,521 or only a total of 169 words that would be "different words" in the New Testament. This is indeed a very, very small number of words, whether 0.4% (562 out of 140,521 words) or 0.12% (169 out of 140,521 words). Dean Burgon's percentage of agreement with the Textus Receptus would be very, very high, whether you take **99.6%** (139,959 out of 140,521 words) or **99.9%** (140,352 out of 140,521 words). So what is all the problem?

(3) The Textus Receptus revision in the "many lesser details" could not be undertaken during Burgon's lifetime because his requirements for the task could not be fulfilled during that time frame.

(4) The Textus Receptus revision in the "many lesser

Chapter I: Dean Burgon & DBS--Both Defending 5

details" must be preceded by at least six major, monumental efforts, most of which have not been fulfilled even in the year 2001 when this book has been written.

(5) **The Dean Burgon Society's Position on the Textus Receptus in View of the Foregoing Is This:** Dean Burgon's requirements were fulfilled neither in the Westcott-Hort Greek text, nor in the Nestle-Aland 26th or 27th edition Greek text, nor in the Hodges-Farstad so-called "Majority Greek Text." Therefore, the Dean Burgon Society is holding firmly to the Textus Receptus that underlies the King James Bible until **all** of Dean Burgon's prerequisites for revision have been fully met! We do so without apology and without fear of logical contradiction!

b. Examples Of Dean Burgon's Views On The Textus Receptus.

(1) **Burgon Esteemed The "Received Text" to Be "Quite Good Enough for All Ordinary Purposes."** He wrote:

". . . essentially the Received Text is full 1550 years old,--(yes, and a vast deal older,)--I esteem it quite good enough for all ordinary purposes. . . ." [Burgon, *REVISION REVISED*, p. 392; available as **#611**, 591 pages for a GIFT of **$25.00+S&H**]

(2) **Burgon Believed The Textus Receptus To Be "An Excellent Text as it Stands, and That the Use of it Will Never Lead Critical Students of Scripture Seriously Astray."** He wrote:

"Obtained from a variety of sources [that is, the Textus Receptus or the Traditional Greek Text] *this text proves to be essentially the same in all. That it requires revision in respect of many of its lesser details is undeniable; but it is at least as certain that it is an excellent text as it stands and that **the use of it will never lead critical students of scripture seriously astray**,--which is what no one will venture to predicate concerning any single critical edition of the N.T. which has been published since the days of Griesbach, by the disciples of Griesbach's school."* [Burgon, *Revision Revised*, p. 269]

(3) **Burgon Estimated The Textus Receptus to Be the True Text "In Nine Cases out of Ten."** He wrote:

*"At least, I will convince every fair person that the truth is what I say it is--viz. that **in nine cases out of ten** the commonly Received Text is the true one."* [Goulburn, *BIOGRAPHY*, Vol. II, p. 278]
For further analysis of this, see section **#2, a, (2)** above, on page 4.

(4) **Burgon Listed Fourteen requirements for any revision of the Textus Receptus Proving Why In His Day Such A Revision Was Impossible**: He wrote:

"Having regard to the Greek text exclusively, we also (strange to relate) had singled out exactly eight from the members of the New

6 Ten Reasons Why DBS Deserves Its Name

Testament company--[1] *divines of un-doubted orthodoxy, who for their* [2] *splendid scholarship and* [3] *proficiency in the best learning,* [4] *might (as we humbly think),* [5] *under certain safeguards, have been* [6] *safely entrusted even with the responsibility of revising the Sacred Text,* [7] *under the guidance of Prebendary Scrivener (who among living Englishmen is facile princeps in these pursuits) it is scarcely anticipated that,* [8] *when unanimous, such Divines* [9] *would ever have materially erred. But then, of course* [10] *a previous* [11] *lifelong familiarity with the science of textual criticism,* [12] *or at least leisure for prosecuting it now, for ten or twenty years,* [13] *with absolutely undivided attention--would be the indispensable requisite for the success of such an undertaking;* [14] *and this, undeniably, is a qualification rather to be desiderated* [that is, "desired"] *than looked for at the hands of English divines of note, in our present day."* [Burgon, *Revision Revised*, pp. 108-9]

(5) Burgon Believed That For an "Authoritative Revision of the Greek Text" They Were "Not Yet Mature" in His Day. He wrote:

*". . . an authoritative revision of the Greek text will have to precede any future revision of the English of the New Testament. Equally certain is it that for such an undertaking, we are **not yet mature**; either in Biblical learning or Hellenistic scholarship."* [Burgon, *Revision Revised*, pp. 124]

(6) Burgon Demanded at Least Six Prerequisites Before Any Authoritative Revision of the Textus Receptus Could Be Successfully Completed. Burgon was writing on page 124 of his book, *Revision Revised*, as quoted in paragraph "(5)" above. After stating that *"for such an undertaking we are not yet mature: either in Biblical learning or Hellenistic scholarship,"* Burgon went on to tell why they were *"not yet mature"* in his day [1883]. It was for the same reasons, we are not yet mature in our day either. These six prerequisites rule out the Nestle-Aland Greek Text (ether the 26th or 27th editions). They also rule out the so-called "Majority Greek Text" of Hodges and Farstad, published by Nelson as we will show later as well as the "Majority Greek Text" of Robinson and Pierpont!

(a) Prerequisite #1: We Need at Least "500 More Copies" of the New Testament "Diligently Collated." Burgon wrote:

"Let 500 more copies. of the Gospels, Acts, and Epistles be diligently collated." [Burgon, *Revision Revised*, p. 125]

This has not yet been done!

(b) Prerequisite #2: We Need at Least "100" "Ancient Lectionaries" "Very Exactly Collated." Burgon wrote:

"Let at least 100 of the ancient Lectionaries be very exactly collated

Chapter I: Dean Burgon & DBS--Both Defending 7

also." [Burgon, *Revision Revised*, p.12 5]
This has not yet been done!

(c) Prerequisite #3: We Need, "Above All," the Church "Fathers" to Yield "Their Precious Secrets" by "Ransacking" Them, "Indexing" Them, and "Diligently Inspecting" Them. Burgon wrote:

"Above all, let the Fathers, be called upon to give up their precious secrets. Let their writings be ransacked and indexed, and (where needful) let the MSS. of their works be diligently inspected in order that we may know what actually is the evidence they afford." [Burgon, *Revision Revised*, p. 125]
This has not yet been done!

(d) Prerequisite #4: We Need the "Most Important of the Ancient Versions" to Be "Edited Afresh" and Let Their "'Languages" Be "Really Mastered by Englishmen." Burgon Wrote:

"Let the most important of the Ancient Versions be edited afresh, and let the languages in which these are written be for the first time really mastered by Englishmen." [Burgon, *Revision Revised*, p. 125]
This has not yet been done!

(e) Prerequisite #5: We Need "Whatever Unpublished Works of the Ancient Greek Fathers" to be "Printed."
Burgon wrote:

"Nay, let whatever unpublished works of the Ancient Greek Fathers are anywhere known to exist,--(and not a few precious remains of theirs are lying hid in great national libraries, both at home and abroad,)--let these be printed. The men could easily be found: the money, far more easily . . . ." [Burgon, *Revision Revised*, pp. 125-26]
This has not yet been done!

(f) Prerequisite #6: We Need "For the First Time" the "Science of Textual Criticism" to Be Prosecuted "In a Scholarlike Manner." Burgon wrote:

"Yes, and in the meantime--(let it in all faithfulness be added)--the science of textual criticism will have to be prosecuted for the first time in a scholarlike manner. Fundamental principles.--sufficiently axiomatic to ensure general acceptance,--will have to be laid down for man's guidance. . . ." [Burgon, *Revision Revised* p.227]
This has not yet been done!

c. Proof That Neither the "Nestle-Aland Greek Text--26th or 27th Edition" Nor the So-called "Majority Greek Text of Hodges-Farstad" Followed Burgon's Six Prerequisites and Are Therefore Not What Burgon Would Call "Authoritative Revisions"

of the Textus Receptus.

(1) The "Nestle-Aland Greek Text--26th or 27th Edition Refused To Follow Burgon's Six Prerequisites and Therefore Is Not What Burgon Would Call an "Authoritative Revision" of the Textus Receptus. If you examine closely the Nestle-Aland Greek Text--26th or 27th edition--in the *Preface*, you will find out a number of things. Using Kurt Aland's 1967 totals for extant Greek manuscript evidence, the edition explains what evidence was used in making up its Greek text. In the first place, there are about 20 Ancient Versions. This figure is derived from the research of Dr. Jack Moorman in his *Early Manuscripts and the Authorized Version--a Closer Look!* [#1825 for a gift of $15.00+S&H], pp. 28-48. The total number of Church Fathers who wrote extensively during the first six centuries was 300, as Burgon has estimated. Here is the evidence used by Nestle-Aland.

The Nestle-Aland Greek Text--26th Edition

1. Papyrus Fragments--   81 out of 81 = 100% of the evidence
2. Uncials--   246 out of 267 = 92% of the evidence
3. Cursives--   202 out of 2764 = 7% of the evidence
4. Lectionaries--   5 out of 2143 = 0.23% of the evidence

Total MSS: 534 out of 5,255 = 10% of the MSS evidence
****

5. Ancient Versions--   3 out of 20 = 15% of the evidence
6. Church Fathers--   72 out of 300 = 24% of the evidence

Total Non-MSS: 75 out of 320 = 23% non-MSS evidence

Grand Total: **609 Out of 5,575 = 11% of ALL evidence**

In the above statistics you will notice that Dean Burgon's prerequisite #1 was not followed. Prerequisite #2 was not followed. Prerequisite #3 was not followed. Prerequisite #4 was not followed. Prerequisite #5 was not followed. Prerequisite #6 was not followed. In fact, Nestle-Aland consistently follows the false principles of Westcott and Hort. Because of this, they group all the so-called Byzantine texts as just one witness. They reject entirely Dean Burgon's methodology in textual criticism. The use of **a mere 10% of the manuscript evidence** is also decidedly against Burgon's sound principles. Nothing short of 100% of the evidence must be used for any major revision of the Textus Receptus that underlies the King James Bible! The same is true of their handling of the non-manuscript evidence of Ancient Versions and Church Fathers. **23% of that evidence is also woefully defective.** Dean Burgon would demand **100% of the evidence** to be used.

Chapter I: Dean Burgon & DBS--Both Defending

(2) **The So-called "Majority Greek Text" of Hodges & Farstad Also Refused to Follow Burgon's Six Prerequisites and Therefore Is Not What Burgon Would Call an "Authoritative Revision"** of the Textus Receptus. If you examine closely the so-called Majority Greek Text of Hodges and Farstad, in the *Preface*, you will find out the following things. Using Kurt Aland's 1967 totals for extant Greek manuscript evidence, the edition makes use of the following evidence. As I said earlier, there are about 20 Ancient Versions according to the research of Dr. Jack Moorman in his *Early Manuscripts and the Authorized Version--a Closer Look!* [#1825 for a gift of $15.00+S&H], pages 28-48. The total number of Church Fathers who wrote extensively during the first six centuries was 300, as Burgon has estimated. Here is the evidence used by Hodges and Farstad.

The So-Called "Majority Greek Text of Hodges-Farstad"

1. Papyrus Fragments--   8 out of 81 = 10% of the evidence
2. Uncials--   4 out of 267 = 1% of the evidence
3. Cursives--   414 out of 2764 = 15% of the evidence
4. Lectionaries--   0 out of 2143 = 0% of the evidence

Total MSS: 426 out of 5,255 = 8% of the MSS evidence

****

5. Ancient Versions--   0 out of 20 = 0% of the evidence
6. Church Fathers--   0 out of 300 = 0% of the evidence

Total Non-MSS: 0 out of 320 = 0% of the non-MSS evidence

Grand Total: **426 out of 5,575 = 7% of ALL evidence**

In the above statistics you will notice that Dean Burgon's prerequisite #1 was not followed. Prerequisite #2 was not followed. Prerequisite #3 was not followed. Prerequisite #4 was not followed. Prerequisite #5 was not followed. Prerequisite #6 was not followed. In fact, the so-called Majority Greek Text of Hodges & Farstad follows the false principles of Westcott and Hort when they refer to **"intrinsic and transcriptional probabilities"** [*Preface*, p. xxii]. The same is true when they make use of the **"genealogical method"** [*Preface*, p. xii] for John 7:53--8:11 and for the book of Revelation. The editors refused to follow completely Dean Burgon's methodology in textual criticism. The use of **a mere 8% of the manuscript evidence** is also decidedly against Burgon's sound principles. Nothing short of **100% of the evidence must be used** for any major revision of the Textus Receptus that underlies the King James Bible!

The same is true of their handling of the non-manuscript evidence of Ancient Versions and Church Fathers. **0% of that evidence is preposterous!** Dean Burgon would demand **100% of this evidence** to be used.

What right does this so-called "Majority Text" and what right does the "Majority Text Society" have in claiming they are following Dean John William Burgon in such a document as this so-called "Majority Greek Text"? To all such people who are under the false impression that this text, is fulfilling the plan, program, and wishes of Dean John William Burgon, let them look again at his **six prerequisites** on pages 6-7 above. Then let them study the above table which shows their use of **only 7% of ALL the evidence** rather than 100% of the present evidence which would fulfill every one of the six prerequisites! Some of those who have this false impression are: (1) Terence Brown (formerly with the Trinitarian Bible Society [TBS] in London; (2) Andrew Brown (formerly with TBS in London); (3) Theodore Letis; (4) Wilbur Pickering; (5) The Majority Text Society, and others. To those who yet have questions about this matter, I would recommend that they order and read two pamphlets: (1) "Seven Defects in the So-called 'Majority Greek Text'" (**#1448**, for a GIFT of **2/$1.50+&H)** and "Why Reject the 'Majority Text.'" (**#1727**, for a GIFT of **2/$1.50+S&H**).

3. Burgon DEFENDED The King James Bible.

a. Burgon Believed the "Men of 1611" Produced "A Work of Real Genius. He wrote:

". . . the plain fact being that the men of 1611--above all that William Tyndale 77 years before them--produced a work of real genius; seizing with generous warmth the meaning and intention of the sacred writers, and perpetually varying the phrase, as they felt or fancied that Evangelists and Apostles would have varied it, had they had to express themselves in English: . . ." [Burgon, *Revision Revised*, p. 167]

b. Burgon Stated That the King James Bible Translators "Understood Their Craft" and That "The Spirit of Their God Was Mightily upon Them." He wrote:

*"Verily, those men **understood their craft**! 'There were giants in those days.' As little would they submit to be bound by the new cords of the Philistines as by their green withes. Upon occasion, they could shake themselves free from either. And why? For the selfsame reason: viz. 'Because **the Spirit of their God was mightily upon them**.'"* [Burgon, *Revision Revised*, p. 196]

c. Burgon Considered the King James Bible to Be "The Noblest Literary Work in the Anglo-Saxon Language. He wrote:

"It may be confidently assumed that no revision of our Authorized Version however judiciously executed, will ever occupy the place in public esteem which is actually enjoyed by the work of the

Chapter I: Dean Burgon & DBS--Both Defending 11

translators of 1611,--the noblest literary work in the Anglo-Saxon language." [Burgon, *Revision Revised*, p. 113]

d. Burgon Would Not "Entertain for a Moment" the Project of Any "Rival Translation" to the King James Bible. Burgon wrote:

*"But certainly only as a handmaid is it to be desired. As something intended to supersede our present English Bible we are thoroughly convinced that the project of a **rival translation** is not to be entertained for a moment. For ourselves, we deprecate* [disappove of] *it entirely."* [Burgon, *Revision Revised*, p. 114]

e. Burgon Thought Any Revision of the King James Bible Should Be in a Way Like "Marginal Notes" or a Similar Way. He wrote:

*"The method of such a performance, whether by **marginal notes** or in some other way, we forbear to determine."* [Burgon, *Revision Revised*, p. 114]

f. Burgon Thought of Any Revision of the King James Bible as Only a "Companion in the Study" for "Private Edification." He wrote:

*"To be brief,--As a **companion in the study** and for **private edification**: as a book of reference for critical purposes, especially in respect of difficult and controverted passages:--we hold that a revised edition of the Authorized Version of our English Bible, (**if** executed with consummate ability and learning,) would at any time be a work of inestimable value."* [Burgon, *Revision Revised*, p. 113--114]

g. Burgon Was Against Any "Future Revision" of the English New Testament until an "Authoritative Revision of the Greek Text Had Been Completed. He wrote:

*"Enough has been offered by this time to prove that an **authoritative revision** of the Greek Text will have to precede any future revision of the English of the New Testament."* [Burgon, *Revision Revised*, p. 124]

4. Burgon Defended the Plenary, Verbal Inspiration and Inerrancy of All Sixty-six Books of the Bible. Before looking at this section of quotations from Dean Burgon, it must be made clear that when he uses the word, "**Bible**," or "**Holy Scripture**," he is referring to the Hebrew/Aramaic and Greek **books, chapters, verses, words, letters, syllables, jots, and tittles** that God breathed out by inspiration and the various human writers wrote down as they were led by the Holy Spirit. **Unless he makes it clear by the context**, he does not refer to any **translation** of that "**Bible**," whether English, Spanish, French, German, or any other language. You should not be confused on this point. Dean Burgon has been misunderstood and misquoted in this very crucial point. Remember, unless otherwise defined, each time Dean Burgon uses the word, "**Bible**" or "**Holy Scripture**," he is referring to the original languages of Hebrew/Aramaic and Greek.

a. Burgon Held That the Very "Words" of the Bible Were "Inspired," and "Every Syllable" as Well. He wrote:

"But if, instead of the 'theory of verbal inspiration,' I am asked whether I believe the words of the Bible to be inspired,--I answer, to be sure I do,--every one of them: and every syllable likewise. Do not you?--Where,--(if it be a fair question,)--Where do you, in your wisdom stop? The book, you allow is inspired. How about the chapters? How about the verses? Do you stop at the verses, and not go on to the words?" [Burgon, *Inspiration and Interpretation*, p. 75]

b. Burgon also believed in plenary, verbal inspiration of "every book" of the Bible. He wrote:

"The Bible (be persuaded) is the very utterance of the Eternal;--as much God's Word, as if high Heaven were open, and we heard God speaking to us with human voice. Every book of it is inspired alike; and is inspired entirely." [Burgon, *Inspiration and Interpretation*, p. 76]

c. Burgon Denied Any "Inspiration" of Any Kind to the "Apocryphal Books." He wrote:

"Inspiration is not a difference of degree, but of kind. The Apocryphal Books are not one atom more inspired than Bacon's Essays." [Burgon, *Inspiration and Interpretation*, p. 76]

d. Burgon Believed That Verbal Inspiration of the Bible Extended down to the "Very Letters." He wrote:

"But the Bible, from the Alpha to the Omega of it, is filled to overflowing with the Holy Spirit of God: the books of it, and the sentences of it, and the words of it, and the syllables of it, aye and the very letters of it."[Burgon, *Inspiration and Interpretation*, p. 76]

e. Burgon Repeated His Firm Belief in the Verbal "Inspiration" of "Every 'Jot' and Every 'Tittle'" of the Bible. He wrote:

"Some here present may remember my repeated and unequivocal assertion that Holy Scripture is inspired from the Alpha to the Omega of it:--not some parts more, some parts less, but all equally, and all to overflowing;--that we hold it to be, not generally inspired but particularly; that we see not how with logical consistency we can avoid believing the words as well as the sentences of it; the syllables as well as the words; the letters as well as the syllables; every 'jot' and every 'tittle' of it (to use our Lord's expression,) to be Divinely inspired: . . ." [Burgon, *Inspiration and Inter-*

Chapter I: Dean Burgon & DBS--Both Defending 13

pretation, p. 94]

f. Burgon Also Believed in the Inerrancy of the Bible since "No Error or Blot of Any Kind Could Possibly Exist Within its Pages." He wrote:

"--and further, that until the contrary has been proved, we shall maintain that no misapprehension or misstatement, no error or blot of any kind, can possibly exist within its pages:--that we hold the Bible to be as much the Word of God, as if God spoke to us therein with human lips;--and that, as the very utterance of the Holy Ghost, we cannot but think that it must be absolute, faultless, unerring, supreme." [Burgon, *Inspiration and Interpretation,* p. 94]

g. Burgon Believed That When You "Read the Bible" You must Believe "That You Are Reading an Inspired Book" Which Is Inspired in Every Part. He wrote, speaking of students at Oxford University who were studying for the ministry:

"And while you read the Bible, read it believing that you are reading an inspired book:--not a book inspired in parts only, but a book inspired in every part:--not a book unequally inspired, but all inspired equally:--not a book generally inspired,--substance indeed given by the Spirit, the words left to the option of the writers; but the words of it as well as the matter of it all--all given by God: As it is written,-- 'Man shall not live by bread alone, but by every word that proceedeth out of the mouth of God.'" [Burgon, *Inspiration and Interpretation,* p. 114]

h. Burgon Did Not Believe Preachers Could "Expound a Text" Unless They Believed "The Words to Be "Inspired." He wrote:

"How can you [that is, the ministerial students at Oxford University] *pretend to expound a text unless you hold the words of that text to be inspired? What inferences can you venture to draw from words, the Divinity of which you dare not affirm?"* [Burgon, *Inspiration and Interpretation,* p. 117]

5. Burgon Defended Against Heresy in His Anglican Church. Apostasy and heresy were present in Dean Burgon's day, even as it is in our own day. Burgon was not a man to be content to sit in silence while apostasy and heresy were permitted within the clergy of his own Church. He felt the heretics should leave the ministry! He did his best to expose them on every occasion possible.

a. Burgon Was a "Watch-dog" Who "Barked Furiously" When Even "The Smallest Danger" Threatened the Church or the Faith. Burgon's biographer, Goulburn, wrote:

"'What a splendid watch-dog he is!' said one in the author's hearing, after perusing and throwing on the table one of the Burgonian

Philippics;--'how loud and furiously he barks when the smallest danger threatens the Church or the Faith which is entrusted to the Church's keeping!' Yes! It is the business of a watch-dog to bark furiously, and even to fly at the throat of pilferers and thieves; and of all pilferers and thieves there are none who more rouse the indignation of honest God-fearing men, than those who would rob the Church of her faith, and the Christian of his hope, by the gradual depredations of rationalism." [Goulburn, *Biography*, Vol. II, p. 67]

    b. **Burgon "Hit His Opponents Rather Hard" Because the "Words of Inspiration" Were "Seriously Imperilled."** He wrote:

"If, therefore, any do complain that I have sometimes hit my opponents rather hard, I take leave to point out that 'to everything there is a season, and a time to every purpose under the sun': 'a time to embrace, and a time to be far from embracing,': a time for speaking smoothly, and a time for speaking sharply. And when the words of inspiration are seriously imperilled, as now they are, it is scarcely possible for one who is determined effectually to preserve the Deposit in its integrity, to hit either too straight or too hard." [Burgon, *Revision Revised*, pp. vii-viii]

    c. **Burgon Thwarted the "Liberal Party" at Oxford University on "More than One Occasion" by His "Unflinching Conservatism."** Goulburn, Dean Burgon's biographer, wrote:

"It is to be wished that it were equally creditable to the government of the day, who seem to have been terrified out of a most suitable appointment by a few disparaging words in Parliament, inspired no doubt by the so-called liberal party in the University [that is, Oxford], *who had been thwarted on more than one occasion by Burgon's stedfast and unflinching conservatism and by his efforts to preserve the connexion of the University with the Church. This party was for revolutionising Oxford; he for reforming it indeed, where it needed reform (had not the new Theological School been established very mainly by his influence?), but always on the old lines."* [Goulburn, *Biography*, Vol. II, p. 136]

    d. **Burgon Preached a Sermon Against the "Disestablishment of Religion" in Oxford Which Was Removing Belief in the Thirty-Nine Articles of Faith.** Goulburn wrote:

"'Your University Tests Bill,' . . . 'is but one of a series of assaults destined to effect an entire separation between the University [that is, Oxford] *and the Church.' . . . 'its effect would be nothing less than the de-Christianizing of the Colleges of Oxford.' . . . the Tests which it abolished were the subscription to the Thirty-Nine Articles,*

Chapter I: Dean Burgon & DBS--Both Defending 15

and the avowal thereby of membership in the Church of England, which hitherto every one, on presenting himself for a degree, had been most properly required to make. This subscription was now required no longer, except in the case of degrees in the Faculty of Divinity." [Goulburn, *Biography*, Vol. II, pp. 178-79]

The above quotations about the "University Tests Bill" were taken from Burgon's sermon on "The Disestablishment of Religion in Oxford, the Betrayal of a Sacred Trust, preached before the University of Oxford; Nov. 21st, 1880 , . . ." [Goulburn, *Biography*, Vol. II, p. 178]

e. Burgon Wrote a Lengthy Criticism of "*Essays and Reviews*" Six of Whose Authors Were "Ministers of the Church of England Who Were Making Light of Their Sacred Profession." He wrote:

"Secondly,--'Essays and Reviews' attracted notice because six of its authors were ministers of the Church of England. Here were six clergymen openly making light of their sacred profession, and apparently worse than regardless of their ordination vows." [Burgon, *Inspiration and Interpretation*, p. xi]

f. Burgon Agreed with an Infidel's Description of the Apostasy Contained in the "*Essays and Reviews*" Which He Refuted. He wrote:

"As an infidel, but certainly in this instance most truthful as well as able Reviewer, remarked concerning the work in question,--'In their ordinary, if not plain sense, there has been discarded the Word of God, the creation, the fall, the redemption, justification, regeneration, and salvation, miracles, inspiration, prophecy, heaven and hell, eternal punishment and a day of judgment, creeds, liturgies, and articles, the truth of Jewish history and Gospel narrative, a sense of doubt thrown over even the incarnation, the resurrection, and ascension, the Divinity of the Second Person, and the Personality of the Third.'" [Burgon, *Inspiration and Interpretation*, p. xi]

This was the nature and the degree of apostasy that Burgon refuted clearly in the beginning pages of his book, *Inspiration and Interpretation*. Remember that six of the seven authors of these *Essays and Reviews* were members of his own Church of England. This did not stop him from exposing their theological errors!

g. Burgon "Handled" the Writers of "*Essays and Reviews*" Just as "Freely" as They "Handled" Divine Truth. He wrote:

"When critics are clamorous for the 'free handling' of Divine Truth, they must not be surprised to find themselves freely handled too. If free discussion is to be the order then let there be free discussion of 'Essays and Reviews,' as well as of the Bible. Six Clergymen of the

Church of England who enter upon a crusade against the Faith of the Church of England must not be astonished if they are looked upon in the light of immoral characters and treated as such. Accordingly, I have handled them as freely as they have handled the Prophets, Apostles, and Evangelists of Christ." [Burgon, *Inspiration and Interpretation*, p. xxvi]

      h. Burgon Identified the Authors of "*Essays and Reviews*" as Being Guilty of "Blasphemy," "Irreligion," and "Infidelity." He wrote:

"*Some respectable persons, I doubt not, will think my treatment of them* [that is, the authors of *"Essays and Reviews"*] *harsh and uncharitable. I invite them to consider that we do not expect blasphemy from Ministers of the Gospel,--irreligion from teachers of youth,--infidelity from the Professor's chair: nor are we called upon to tolerate it either.*" [Burgon, *Inspiration and Interpretation*, p. xxiv]

      i. Burgon Believed "Essays and Reviews" Sapped the "Foundation of Faith." He wrote:

[Referring to *Essays and Reviews*] "*. . . a volume, the confessed tendency of which is to sap the foundation of Faith and to introduce irreligion with a flood-tide.*" [Burgon, *Inspiration and Interpretation*, p. xxiv]

      j. Burgon Did Not Think "Punctilious Courtesy" Should Be Practiced in Denouncing Those Who Handle the Things of God in an Outrageous Manner." He wrote:

"[Burgon was going] *mercilessly to uncover their baseness, and uncompromisingly to denounce it. If I may declare my mind freely, punctilious courtesy in dealing with such opinions, becomes a species of treason against Him after whose Name we are called, and whom we profess to serve. Seven men may combine to handle the things of God, it seems, in the most outrageous manner; while themselves are to be the objects of consideration, tenderness, respect! I cannot see their title to any consideration at all.*" [Burgon, *Inspiration and Interpretation*, p. xxiv]

      k. Burgon Exposed His Church's Clergymen Who Denied the "Fact of Our Lord's Resurrection" as the Worst Enemies of Christ. He wrote:

"*Will men try to persuade us that the <u>idea</u> of our Lord's resurrection is a more secure basis for the Church's Faith than the <u>fact</u> of our Lord's resurrection? . . . Not only will I <u>not</u> treat men with tenderness who put forth such blasphemous folly, . . . but I will hold them up to ridicule, to the very utmost of my power. Nay, I would make them objects of unqualified reprobation to all, if I could as*

Chapter I: Dean Burgon & DBS--Both Defending 17

they deserve, for they are the worst enemies of the Gospel of Christ." [in his footnote, Burgon stated: *"I have softened the expression originally employed in this place, out of deference to the opinions of some wise and good men. But I do not think that St. John, (the Evangelist and Apostle of Dogma,) would have thought my language too strong: nor St. Paul either."*] [Burgon, *Inspiration and Interpretation*, pp. 248-49]

l. Burgon Urged His Fellow Anglican Clergymen Who Were Heretics to "Recall Their Words" or "Resign Their Stations." He wrote:
[Speaking of the writers of the *Essays and Reviews*] *"They must first withdraw from the cause which they have betrayed, cease to profess the teaching which they have disbelieved, resign their commission in a Church to whose doctrine and discipline they openly proclaim themselves to be opposed. . . . they cannot imagine, for a moment, that, as honest men, they can remain where they are! They must either recall their words or resign their stations."* [Burgon, *Inspiration and Interpretation*, p. xxviii]

6. Burgon Defended Against the Heresy of Romanism and "Romanizing Practices" Within His Church. Some uninformed writers have set forth the absurd and inaccurate information to the effect that Burgon was in favor of Romanizing tendencies within his Anglican Church and that he agreed with the Oxford Movement of Pusey and Newman. Nothing could be further from the truth as these quotations will show very clearly!

a. Burgon "Abhorred" "Romanism." He wrote:
"I see further that if I had a parish in London, I should stand almost alone.--Romanism I abhor." [Goulburn, *Biography*, Vol. I, p. 186]

b. Burgon "Condemned Entirely" the Roman Catholic Error of "Prayer for the Dead." He wrote:
"Prayer for the dead in the sense of a prayer that their ultimate doom, for weal or for woe, may be reversed--or even mitigated--is a 'fond conceit,' finding countenance neither in Scripture nor in antiquity. I condemn it entirely." [Goulburn, *Biography*, Vol. II, p. 246]

c. Burgon Was Opposed to Either "Ritualism" or "Romanising Practices" in His Church. Here's a quote from a letter of August 23, 1889, to Burgon's biographer, Goulburn:
"You ask me about Burgon in Convocation . . . . He brought with him strongly his dislike to that 'thing called ritualism.' I remember one occasion, on which he pointed with a distinctness which could not be mistaken, to our encouraging Romanising practices." [Goulburn, *Biography*, Vol. II, 77, 194]

d. Burgon Protested Strongly Against a "Florid Ritual" Which Made "Communion" Similar to the "Roman Mass." Burgon's biographer, Goulburn, wrote:
"But his letter to the Archbishop was only the precursor of a much lengthier and more substantial protest, which later in this same year Burgon made against the introduction into the Church of England of a florid ritual, utterly unauthorised, as he thought, by the Book of Common Prayer, or rather condemned by it, when fairly and reasonably interpreted, and the tendency and effect of which was to assimilate the service of the holy communion as closely as possible to the Roman mass." [Goulburn, *Biography*, Vol. II, p. 189]

e. Burgon Opposed "Romanising and Ritualising Tendencies" in His Church as Well as "Rationalism Which Was Undermining the Faith." Goulburn wrote:
"The close of this year gave Burgon occasion to declare himself as much opposed to the Romanising and ritualising tendencies in the Church as he had hitherto showed himself to be to the rationalism which was slowly on all sides undermining the faith, and derogating from the honour and perfection of God's Holy Word." [Goulburn, *Biography*, Vol. II, p. 84]

f. Burgon Was So Much Against "Romanizing" of His Church That He Preached Two Sermons Against it in 1873. Goulburn wrote:
"On Wednesday and Thursday, the 1st and 2nd of October, in the year 1873, was held the Oxford Diocesan Conference, the proceedings of which elicited from Burgon two sermons, preached on the 12th and 19th of the month, and published by him with a word of Preface dated on the 28th." [Goulburn, *Biography*, Vol. II, p. 84]

A footnote gives more information on the two sermons. They were entitled: "The Oxford Diocesan Conference; and Romanizing [*sic*] Within the Church of England: two Sermons preached by John W. Burgon, B.D., Vicar of St. Mary the Virgin's, Fellow of Oriel College, and Gresham Lecturer in Divinity." [Goulburn, *Biography*, Vol. II, p. 84]

g. Burgon Repudiated the Two Resolutions Made by the Oxford Diocesan Conference Which Furthered the Romanising Movement Within the Church of England." Goulburn summed up Burgon's repudiation of the Conference:
"Burgon explains that to both these resolutions he personally entertained the strongest repugnance: but he discerns underlying both of them (and there is no doubt he was right in his discernment) the 'growing impatience of the faithful laity at the Romanising movement within the Church of England, which is even now making its way in many quarters unrestrained, and even unrebuked' [p. 12];

Chapter I: Dean Burgon & DBS--Both Defending

in the second sermon, 'taking up a position directly hostile to many of my personal friends' [preface, p. 5]; he launches out with his usual plain speaking and intrepidity against the Romanising practices and tenets which were being introduced and inculcated; against the representing tradition as an unwritten word, of co-ordinate authority with the written [p. 18]; against saint worship and Mariolatry [p. 19]; against enforced habitual auricular confession [pp. 77] against transubstantiation, and all the observances and ceremonial in connexion with the Holy Communion which are grouped round transubstantiation, such as vestments, the eastward position, fasting, communion, and non-communicating attendance, as well as the phraseologies unknown to our own Book of Common Prayer, such as high mass and low mass [pp. 22, 23]. . . ." [Goulburn, *Biography*, Vol. II, p. 85]

h. Burgon Preached Against the "Ritualists" and Various "Romish Doctrines" Which He Called "Mediaevalism in the Church of England." Goulburn wrote:

"Burgon preached before the University [of Oxford] his sermon on 'Nehemiah, a Pattern to Builders' . . . The burning question was the revival of mediaevalism in the Church of England by the ritualists, their distortion of the proportions of the Faith by exclusively dwelling upon the doctrine of the Holy Eucharist 'as if it were the sum and substance of all Divinity,' and their industrious advocacy of the 'Romish doctrine of confession.' As the 'lighted candles and incense and birettas, and the use of the chasuble,'--Burgon 'cannot away with them;--'the masculine vigour which the severe study of Scripture imparts to a well trained mind must produce a recoil from all such trumpetry, an utter revulsion of mind.' It was the old, old story which he had heard so often before,--that the Bible, studied as a whole furnishes the sufficient refutation of all religious error, whether ritualistic or rationalistic." [Goulburn, *Biography*, Vol. II, pp. 160-161]

7. Burgon Defended Against the Errors of the English Revised Version of 1881 and the Underlying Greek Text. He wrote an entire book entitled *Revision Revised*, one third of which pointed out the many, many errors of the English Revised Version of 1881 itself, and two thirds of which repudiated both the Greek Text and the theory behind the Text that underlay it. Just two quotes will suffice for our purposes here.

a. Burgon Believed the ERV's "Revision of the Sacred Text" Was "Untrustworthy from Beginning to End." He wrote:

"My one object has been to defeat the mischievous attempt which

was made in 1881 to thrust-upon this Church and realm a revision of the Sacred Text, which--recommended though it be by eminent names--I am thoroughly convinced, and am able to prove, is untrustworthy from beginning to end. The reason is plain. It has been constructed throughout on an utterly erroneous hypothesis." [Burgon, *Revision Revised*, pp. v-vi]

b. Burgon Felt He Had "Crushed the Revised Version" of 1881 So it Would "Never Lift up its Head Again." He wrote:

"*'One thing, however,' he continued after a short pause, 'is a consolatory reflexion, that I have been enabled to crush the Revised Version of the New Testament, so that I believe it will never lift up its head again.'*" [Goulburn, *Biography*, Vol. II, p. 291]

B. As Dean Burgon, the Dean Burgon Society Is a Defending Society.

1. The Dean Burgon Society Motto Is "In Defense of Traditional Bible Texts." The very motto which appears on our Dean Burgon Society seal shows that we are definitely a **Defending** Society.

2. As Dean Burgon, the Dean Burgon Society Defends the "Masoretic Hebrew Text." The Dean Burgon Society "*Articles of Faith, Operation & Organization*" state clearly: "*We believe that the texts which are the closest to the original autographs of the Bible are the Traditional Masoretic Hebrew Text for the Old Testament, . . .*" [DBS *Articles of Faith*, p. 2]

3. As Dean Burgon, the Dean Burgon Society Defends the "Textus Receptus." The DBS "*Articles of Faith*" state: "*We believe that the texts which are the closest to the original autographs of the Bible are the . . Traditional Greek Text for the New Testament underlying the King James Version (as found in 'The Greek Text Underlying The English Authorized Version of 1611' as published by the Trinitarian Bible Society in 1976).*" [DBS *Articles of Faith*, pp. 2-3]

4. As Dean Burgon, the DBS Defends the King James Bible. The DBS "*Articles of Faith* states: "*We believe that the King James Version or Authorized Version of the English Bible is a true, faithful, and accurate translation of these two providentially preserved texts, which in our time has no equal among all of the other English Translations. The translators did such a fine job in their translation task that we can without apology hold up the Authorized Version of 1611 and say, 'This is the Word*

Chapter I: Dean Burgon & DBS--Both Defending 21

of God!' while at the same time realizing that, in some verses, we must go back to the underlying original language Texts for complete clarity, and also compare Scripture with Scripture." "We believe that all the verses in the King James Version belong in the Old and the New Testaments because they represent words we believe were in the original texts, although there might be other renderings from the original languages which could also be acceptable to us today. For an exhaustive study of any of the words or verses in the Bible, we urge the student to return directly to the Traditional Masoretic Hebrew Text and the Traditional Received Greek Text rather than to any other translation for help." [DBS *Articles of Faith*, p. 3]

5. As Dean Burgon, the DBS Defends the Plenary, Verbal Inspiration and Inerrancy of All Sixty-six Books of the Bible. The DBS *"Articles of Faith"* state:

"We believe in the plenary verbal divine inspiration of the sixty-six canonical books of the Old and the New Testaments (from Genesis to Revelation) in the original languages and their consequent infallibility and inerrancy in all matters of which they speak (2 Timothy 3:16-17; 2 Peter 1:21; 1 Thessalonians 2:13). The books known as the Apocrypha, however, are not the Inspired Word of God in any sense whatsoever." [DBS *Articles of Faith*, p. 2]

6. As Dean Burgon, the DBS Defends Against the Heresy of Romanism. The DBS *Articles of Faith* do not have any specific statement concerning "Romanism" as such, but throughout these "*Articles*," the heresy of Romanism is precluded. [Cf. DBS *Articles of Faith*, pp. 2-6]

7. As Dean Burgon, the DBS Defends Against Westcott and Hort's Greek Text. The Dean Burgon Society's *Articles of Faith* lists 13 "objects." Object #4 states:

"4. To defend the Traditional Received Greek Text which underlies the King James Version (as found in 'The Greek Text Underlying The English Authorized Version of 1611' as published by the Trinitarian Bible Society in 1976." [DBS *Articles of Faith*, p. 7]

This rules out "Westcott and Hort's" Greek text. Object #6 states:

"6. To expose and publicize the defects, deficiencies, errors, and mistakes both in the texts used and in the translation process and results of any and all modern translations of the Bible, whether in English, or in other languages, which are not based on the Traditional Masoretic Hebrew Text and Traditional Received Greek Text which underlie the King James Version." [DBS *Articles of Faith*, p. 7]

Again, this rules out the "Westcott and Hort's" Greek Text. Object #7 states in part:

"... *Further, it shall be our purpose to keep abreast of future bibliographic offerings in order to criticize and warn against those deviating from the Traditional Masoretic Hebrew Text and the Traditional Received Text which underlie the King James Version.*" [DBS *Articles of Faith*, p. 7]

This also discards "Westcott and Hort's" Greek text.

8. As Dean Burgon, the DBS Defends Against the English Revised Version of 1881. Object #6 speaks to this:

"*6. To expose and publicize the defects, deficiencies, errors, and mistakes both in the texts used and in the translation process and results of any and all modern translations of the Bible, whether in English, or in other languages, which are not based on the Traditional Masoretic Hebrew Text and Traditional Received Greek Texts which Underlie the King James Version.*" [DBS *Articles of Faith*, p. 7]

Object #5 states:

"*5. To defend the Traditional English Translation of the Bible--the King James Version (or Authorized Version)--as a true, faithful, and accurate translation from the underlying original Texts which have been providentially preserved for us, which Translation has no equal in our time among all of the other English translations.*" [DBS *Articles of Faith*, p. 7]

This certainly includes the English Revised Version (ERV) as being inferior to the King James Bible.

CHAPTER II
AS DEAN BURGON, THE DEAN BURGON SOCIETY IS AN EDUCATIONAL SOCIETY

A. Dean Burgon Was An EDUCATIONAL Individual.

1. Burgon EDUCATED By Writing His Many Books On The Traditional Text. Dean Burgon's books on the Traditional Greek Text which have been reprinted by the Dean Burgon Society are five in number: (1) *The Revision Revised* (#611 for a GIFT of $25.00 +S&H); (2) *Inspiration and Interpretation* (#1220 for a GIFT of $25.00+S&H); (3) *The Last Twelve Verses of Mark* (#1139 for a GIFT of $15.00+S&H); (4) *The Traditional Text of the Holy Gospels* (#1159 for a GIFT of $16.00+S&H); and (5) *Causes of Corruption of the Holy Gospels* (#1160 for a GIFT of $15.00+S&H). These are powerful **EDUCATIONAL** tools which should be owned and read by everyone!

2. Burgon EDUCATED By Training Men For The Ministry. Burgon was greatly used in his day in the preparation and training of what we call today, "preacher boys," in his own denomination. He held a post at Oxford University for many years as well as being an active Pastor. The last half of his book, *Inspiration and Interpretation*, is a series of lectures about the Word of God to young men at Oxford who were studying for the ministry.

B. As DEAN BURGON. The DEAN BURGON SOCIETY Is An EDUCATIONAL Society.

1. The Dean Burgon Society EDUCATES By Its DBS News. Since its founding in 1978, the Dean Burgon Society has published from time to time the *Dean Burgon News*. This is an educational venture, going to many individuals, pastors, and school libraries.

2. The Dean Burgon Society EDUCATES by its Printed Pamphlets. Through the years of its existence, the DBS has published the following pamphlets and/or booklets: (1) *The Articles of Faith, Operation & Organization* (#958, 16 pp.); (2) *Bible Preservation* (#1389, 8 pp.); (3) *Defects in the So-called "Majority" Greek Text* (#1448, 16 pp.); (4) *Defects in the New King James Version* (#1465, 28 pp.); (5) *The K.J.V. 1611 Compared to the Present K.J.V.* (#1495, 12 pp.); (6) *Defects in the New*

American Standard Version (#**1518**, 38 pp.); (*7) How We Got Our Bible* (#**1562**, 38 pp.); (8) *Why Reject the "Majority Text"* (#**1727**, 16 pp.); (9) *Awana Churches--Keep Using the 'Old King James'* (#**1738**, 40 pp.); (10) *Awana's Errors in Leaving Their King James Bible Stand* (#**1823**, 24 pp.); and (11) *Defects in the New International Version* (#**2054**, 38 pp.). These are all available from the Dean Burgon Society for the asking. Gifts would be appreciated.

3. The Dean Burgon Society EDUCATES By Its Annual Meetings On Audio And Video Cassettes and Message Book. Each year, during our Dean Burgon Society annual meetings, the messages are recorded on both audio and video cassettes, and are made available to anyone who wants to hear and/or see them. Most of these messages are then compiled into an annual DBS Message Book. This is certainly an **EDUCATIONAL** ministry. We do get requests for the tapes, videos, and Message Book each year so that people can learn from the DBS messages.

4. The Dean Burgon Society EDUCATES By Its "Articles of Faith." The Dean Burgon Society's *ARTICLES OF FAITH, OPERATION & ORGANIZATION* is an educational pamphlet in and of itself. It gives information about the DBS such as: (1) Our Name; (2) Our *Articles of Faith* on (a) The Bible; (b) The Trinity; (c) The Person Of Christ; (d) The Birth of Christ; (e) The Death of Christ; (f) The Resurrection Of Christ; (g) Salvation; (h) Heaven and Hell; (i) Spiritual Unity; (j) Purity of the Church; (k) Separation; (1) Creation; (3) Our Purpose and Object, including 13 different Objects; (4) Our Membership; (5) Our Officers and Administration, including (a) Titled Officers; (b) Executive Committee Officers; (6) Our Finances; (7) Our Parliamentary Authority; (8) Our Meetings; (9) Our Prayer and Praise; (10) Our Tax-Exempt Provisions and the Dissolution of the Society; and (11) Our Amendments. This is **Educational** throughout.

5. The Dean Burgon Society EDUCATES By Making Over 1,000 Titles Available In Defense of the King James Bible And Its Underlying Texts. As of this writing, there are a total of over 1,000 titles available through the Dean Burgon Society and/or the Bible for Today defending both the King James Bible and its underlying Hebrew and Greek Texts. These consist of books (both old reprints, and current volumes), articles, pamphlets, tracts, audio cassettes, and video cassettes. Certainly this is **EDUCATIONAL.**

CHAPTER III
AS DEAN BURGON, THE DEAN BURGON SOCIETY IS AN ADAMANT SOCIETY

A. Dean Burgon Was An ADAMANT Individual.
   1. Burgon was ADAMANT In His Refusal to Compromise in General.
      a. **Burgon Refused to Compromise In General By Sticking to His Colours.** Goulburn quoted from Dean Burgon's letter to a young fellow student. He wrote:
   "Anyhow, our course is clear. Through good and ill report to stick to our colours, praying for sweet tempers and strong hearts (if need be): advancing nothing one does not feel sure of: and when once advanced, dying rather than recalling . I am inclined to think with you, that a fiery trial is at hand." [Goulburn, *Biography*, Vol. I, p. 148]
      b. **Burgon Refused To Compromise In General By Delivering Himself with Courage.** Goulburn wrote of Burgon:
   "For his trumpet gave no uncertain sound, and on all great questions as they arose,--and there were many,--he delivered himself with courage, as one who was convinced himself and strove to convince others." [Goulburn, *Biography*, Vol. II, p. 405]
      c. **Burgon Refused To Compromise In General By His "INDOMITABLE FORCE OF WILL."** Goulburn wrote:
   ". . . the character [of Burgon] *itself was one of great originality, with a vivid colour, and an indomitable force of will all its own. This force of will which gave him a tenacity of purpose in carrying into effect everything he undertook, by its very unyieldedness failed entirely to carry others with it. Compromise was a word unknown to him . . . and therefore he stood and acted alone and never had (as indeed he never cared to have) a following among his equals."* [Goulburn, *Biography*, Vol. I, p. xii).
      d. **Burgon Refused To Compromise In General By His Obvious "Sincerity."** Goulburn wrote:
   "There could never be a doubt of Dean Burgon's sincerity. It was written in his very looks, as it found expression in his words, in his writings, [and] his actions." [Goulburn, Biography, Vol. II, 403]

2. Burgon was ADAMANT In His Refusal to Compromise on the Word of God.

a. Burgon Refused To Compromise On The Word Of God By "Maintaining the Integrity of the Written Word of God." Burgon's biographer, Goulburn, wrote:

"Burgon was in this country the leading religious teacher of his time, who brought all the resources of genius and profound theological learning to rebut the encroachments of rationalism by maintaining inviolate the integrity of the written Word of God as the Church has received it . . ." [Goulburn, *Biography*, Vol. I, p. 1]

b. Burgon Refused to Compromise On The Word Of God By His "Burning Zeal" For It. Goulburn wrote:

"Burgon exhibited in his reply a crowning specimen of that burning zeal for God's Truth, and that splendid uncompromising intrepidity and outspokenness, which characterized all his controversial efforts." [Goulburn, *Biography*, Vol. II, p. 272]

c. Burgon Refused To Compromise On The Word Of God By Maintaining "A Burning Zeal for the Word of God" as a Champion in a Cause. Goulburn quoted from the Pastor who delivered Burgon's funeral sermon. He wrote:

"It was his burning zeal for the Word of God which stirred him to come forward as a champion in a cause which he thought was being betrayed by those who should have been its guardians." [Goulburn, *Biography*, Vol. II, p. 405]

d. Burgon Refused To Compromise On The Word Of God By His "Reverence" For It. Goulburn wrote:

"No part of his character was more remarkable than his reverence for the Word of God." [Goulburn, *Biography*, Vol. II, p. 403]

e. Burgon Refused To Compromise On The Word Of God By "Treasuring" it as "Infinitely Precious." Goulburn wrote:

"Every jot and tittle of the Scriptures was infinitely precious to him. He treasured them not as the word of man, but the Word of God, given by a real, immediate inspiration, and communicated to His servants, Prophets, Evangelists, Apostles, each in his own good time." [Goulburn, Biography, Vol. II, p. 406]

B. As Dean Burgon, the Dean Burgon Society Is an Adamant Society.

1. As Dean Burgon, the DBS Is Adamant in Its Refusal To Compromise In General. The Dean Burgon Society has showed that it is **ADAMANT** in its general doctrinal tenacity. There are not very many organizations at take all of the firm stands in doctrine: (1) The eternal Sonship of the Lord Jesus Christ (Article II, C, p. 4); (2) The power of

Chapter III: Dean Burgon & DBS--Both Adamant

Christ's redeeming Blood (Article II, E, p. 5); (3) The Biblical separation from both apostasy and from "disorderly" brethren (Article ii, k, p. 6); and (4) the direct creation by God of the universe and of man in six literal solar days (Article ii, l, p. 6). It would be difficult to find very many organizations that are clear on all four of these above doctrinal distinctives--especially since each of them is under severe attack in our days! The DBS is **ADAMANT** in the defense of each one of them!

2. As Dean Burgon, the DBS Is ADAMANT In Its Stand On The Texts and Translations Of The Bible.

Though the above paragraph sets the Dean Burgon Society off as a separatist and Fundamentalist Society without ties either to the apostasy or to neo-evangelical compromises, it is basically a one-issue society! As such, it takes an **ADAMANT** stance on the following things:

(1) **We believe** the Bible is infallible and inerrant in all matters of which it speaks. This is unlimited inerrancy (Article II, A, p. 2).

(2) **We believe** the original language texts which have been providentially preserved and the closest to the original autographs of the Bible are the Traditional Masoretic Hebrew Text for the Old Testament and the Traditional Greek Text for the New Testament which texts were the texts used as the source for the King James Bible (Article II, A, pp. 2-3).

(3) **We believe** the King James Bible is a true and accurate translation of these two providentially preserved texts which has no equal among all of the other English translations (Article II, A, p. 3).

(4) **We believe** the King James Bible is such a fine translation we can without apology hold it up and say "This is the Word of God" in English! (Article II, A, p. 3).

(5) **We believe** all the verses in the King James Bible belong there because they represent words that were in the original Texts (Article II, A, p. 3).

(6) **We believe** that for an exhaustive study of any of the words or verses in the Bible, we urge the student to return directly to the Traditional Masoretic Hebrew Text and the Traditional Received Greek Text rather than to any other translation for help (Article II, A, p. 3).

(7) **We believe** Dean Burgon's books and others of a similar nature should be reprinted and circulated (Article III, B, 1, pp. 6-7).

(8) **We believe** the Traditional Masoretic Hebrew Text of the Old Testament that underlies the King James Bible must be defended (Article III, B, 3, p. 7).

(9) **We believe** the Traditional Received Greek Text of the New Testament which underlies the King James Bible must be defended (Article III, B, 4, p. 7).

(10) **We believe** the Traditional English Translation of the Bible--

the King James Version (or Authorized Version) must be defended as a true, faithful, and accurate translation from the underlying original Texts which have been providentially preserved for us, which Translation has no equal in our time among all of the other English "Translations" (Article III, B, 5, p. 7).

(11) We believe we must expose and publicize the defects, deficiencies, errors, and mistakes both in the Texts used and in the Translation process and results of any and all modern translations of the Bible, whether in English, or in other languages, which are NOT based on the Traditional Masoretic Hebrew Text and Traditional Received Greek Text which underlie the King James Bible (Article III, B, 6, p. 7).

(12) We believe we should especially analyze the so-called "Majority Greek Text" of Zane Hodges and reply thereto (Article III, B, 7, p. 7).

(13) We believe we should criticize and warn against any future bibliographic offerings deviating from the Traditional Masoretic Hebrew Text and the Traditional Received Greek Text which underlie the King James Bible. (Article III, B, 7, p. 7).

(14) We believe we should revive interest in the firsthand study of the Hebrew and Greek Text of the Bible by the three general means indicated in the "Articles of Faith" (Article III, B, 8, p. 8).

(15) We believe we should acquire, print, sell, and distribute other sound books by the scholars who lived around the time of Dean John William Burgon who defended the Traditional Masoretic Hebrew Text, the Traditional Received Greek Text, and the King James Bible, giving sound reasons why these Texts and this Version should be accepted as the best (Article III, B, 9, p. 8).

(16) We believe we should acquire, sell, and distribute English Scriptures in the King James Version, and translations in other languages which are based solely and exclusively on the Traditional Masoretic Hebrew Text and the Traditional Received Greek Texts which underlie the King James Bible(Article III, B, 10, p. 8).

(17) We believe we should encourage articles, research, books, and other materials devoted to the study of the history, canon, text, authority, inspiration, and translation of the Bible (Article III, B, 11, p. 8).

(18) We believe we should inform believers about the danger of using and recommending Bibles which, while claiming to be the King James Bible, actually make changes in the text (Article III, B, 12, pp. 8-9).

(19) We believe we should encourage the most careful scrutiny of Bibles published in languages other than English which deviate from the Traditional Masoretic Hebrew Text and the Traditional Received Greek Text which underlie the King James Bible (Article III, B, 12, p. 9).

(20) We believe we should organize, write, edit, publish, and circulate widely a "Newsletter" which will concentrate on the various objectives

Chapter III: Dean Burgon & DBS—Both Adamant 29

of the Society listed in its "*Articles of Faith*" and those additional objectives which might be determined from time to time (Article III, B, 13, p. 9).

CHAPTER IV
AS DEAN BURGON, THE DEAN BURGON SOCIETY IS A NEGLECTED SOCIETY

A. Dean Burgon Was A NEGLECTED Individual.

1. Burgon was NEGLECTED By His Not Being On The English Revised Version (ERV) Of 1881. Though eminently qualified, Dean Burgon was not chosen by his Anglican Church to sit on the revision committee when the English Revised Version (ERV) was made. Dr. Scrivener was about the only conservative on that committee who knew well the intricacies of textual criticism. Burgon would have made an excellent member of that team. He was not selected, however, but was **NEGLECTED**! Perhaps this was due to Burgon's strong and fearless faith and belief in the inerrancy of every Word of God together with his battle with members of his own church who were leaning toward apostasy.

2. Burgon was NEGLECTED By His Being Attacked Or Laughed At. In many of the contemporary books, including his own biography, Burgon was attacked or laughed at in some way or another. Present day writers either neglect him entirely, or else seem to imply that his writings were sharp and much too belligerent. I have read five books of his on textual criticism, and find his words most appropriate for the occasion. He had a serious mission of the defense of the imperilled words and even letters of Scripture, so he laid out his arguments in straightforward, hard-hitting terms, appropriate for his subject matter.

3. Burgon was NEGLECTED By Not Being Elevated To Anglican Bishop, Only To Dean. In Burgon's day, as in our own, there was much political influence brought to bear on Anglican appointments to the office of Bishop. In fact, church politics existed then, as now, in virtually all of the churches. Burgon was "passed over" for important promotions because of his exposure of apostasy within his own church as well as his courageous stand for the Traditional Text of the New Testament in opposition to the spurious Greek text of Westcott and Hort.

B. As DEAN BURGON, The DEAN BURGON SOCIETY Is A NEGLECTED Society.

1. As Dean Burgon, The DBS Is NEGLECTED By

Chapter IV: Dean Burgon & DBS--Both Adamant   31

Being Little Known. We are not in all the news magazines, either secular or Christian. Probably very few of those in the media even know of our existence since 1978. That's all right. We try the best we can to make our cause known. We'll be content to let the Lord make our cause known as, and when, He sees fit. We have had ads in the *Sword of the Lord* from time to time which had some very good response. We might have some more, as the Lord gives us the funds. We are advertised on several radio stations both for thirty minutes each week and five minutes per day. We have some schools and colleges who subscribe for their libraries to our *Dean Burgon News*--even some that are neo-evangelical and even liberal. This is surprising, is it not? They don't take our position, yet they want to know what it is! But by and large, DBS is **NEGLECTED** by being little known.

2. As Dean Burgon, The DBS Is NEGLECTED By Being Attacked, Set Aside, and Laughed at. The DBS is attacked by the Westcott and Hort group of Christians (even by Fundamentalists) since we are the so-called "Textus Receptus Text" group of Christians. All such attacks are answered by truth and facts. We go right on our way, standing for the truth as it is in the Traditional Masoretic Hebrew Text, the Traditional Received Greek Text, and the Traditional English King James Bible. We are not deterred by any attack.

CHAPTER V
AS DEAN BURGON, THE DEAN BURGON SOCIETY IS A BELIEVING SOCIETY

A. Dean Burgon Was A BELIEVING Individual.

1. Burgon was A BELIEVING Individual By Holding To The Plenary, Verbal Inspiration of The Bible. Throughout his book on *Inspiration and Interpretation* (available as #1220 for a GIFT of $25.00+S&H), Dean Burgon spelled out in great detail his unshakable belief in the plenary, verbal inspiration of the Bible. In fact, he believed every letter of the Bible was inspired. Such strong belief was entirely absent from Westcott and Hort, his contemporaries.

2. Burgon was A BELIEVING Individual By Urging The Reading Of The Bible From Genesis To Revelation. Certainly a man would not advocate reading through the Bible from Genesis to Revelation as Dean Burgon did unless he really **BELIEVED** in it. He knew firsthand the power of the Bible, the Word of God. This is found also in *Inspiration and Interpretation*.

3. Burgon was A BELIEVING Individual By Holding To The Creation Of The World In Six Literal Days. Goulburn, his biographer, wrote:

"*I insist on taking everything in this Chapter of Genesis quite literally. I cannot even suffer it to be called a poem or a psalm. It is neither. . . . But Genesis I is very severe, very unadorned prose. It purports to be, and undoubtedly it is, history in the strictest sense; revealed history, and therefore true history. It claims to be and it certainly is the history of six ordinary days.*" [Goulburn, *Biography*, Vol. II, p. 248]

Dean Burgon had no doubts about the literal nature of creation. His biographer wrote:

"*The Book of Genesis, like the Acts of the Apostles, was a favourite Book with him. The simple but most stately and majestic record of Creation, to the acceptance of which in its literal and obvious sense--the sense in which a child would accept it,--he clung (as we shall see) to the last moment of his life.*" [Goulburn, *Biography*, Vol. II,

Chapter V: Dean Burgon & DBS–Both Believing

p. 16]
Dean Burgon had no patience whatever with the "Darwinian Theory" of evolution. Goulburn wrote:

"Natural Science In Their Relation To The Christian Faith;--in which a qualified assent was given to the doctrine of evolution. Burgon's reply to him, showing both his affectionate feeling to his friends of Auld Lang Syne, and his abhorrence of the Darwinian Theory will be found among the letters appended to this year." [Goulburn, *Biography*, Vol. II, p. 2201.

4. Burgon was A BELIEVING Individual By Trusting In The "Blood" of Christ For Salvation. Goulburn stated:

". . . in looking back upon it, my past life yields nothing that is satisfactory to me, and that I have no hope but in the blood and grace of our Divine Lord." [Goulburn, *Biography*, Vol. II, p. 291]

B. As Dean Burgon, the Dean Burgon Society Is A BELIEVING Society.

1. As Dean Burgon, The DBS Is BELIEVING In The Plenary, Verbal Inspiration Of The Bible. The *Articles of Faith* of the DBS state clearly:

"We believe in the plenary, verbal, divine inspiration of the sixty-six canonical books of the Old and the New Testament (from Genesis to Revelation) in the original languages, and in their consequent infallibility and inerrancy in all matters of which they speak (2 Timothy 3:16-17; 2 Peter 1:21; 1 Thessalonians 2:13)." [DBS *Articles of Faith*, Section II, paragraph A, p. 2]

2. As Dean Burgon, The DBS Is BELIEVING In The Reading of and The Power Of The Bible. The *Articles of Faith* of the DBS mention:

"The translators [of the King James Bible] *did such a fine job in their translation task that we can without apology hold up the Authorized Version of 1611 and say 'This is the Word of God!' while at the same time realizing that, in some verses, we must go back to the underlying original language texts for complete clarity, and also compare Scripture with Scripture."* [DBS *Articles of Faith*, Section 11, paragraph A, p. 3]

3. As Dean Burgon, The DBS Is BELIEVING By Holding To The Creation Of The World In Six Literal Days. The *Articles of Faith* of the DBS state:

"L. Creation. We believe in the Biblical account of the creation of the entire universe, angels, and man; that this account is neither allegory nor myth, but a historical account of the direct, immediate

creative acts of God in six literal solar days without any evolutionary process, either naturalistic or theistic; . . ." [DBS *Articles of Faith*, Section II, paragraph L, p. 6]

4. As Dean Burgon, The DBS Is BELIEVING In The "Blood" Of Christ To Save. The *Articles of Faith* of the DBS state: *"E. The Death of Christ. We believe in Christ's substitutionary, propitiatory, expiatory, vicarious death, and in the atoning power of His redeeming blood. 'Ye were not redeemed with corruptible things . . . but with the precious blood of Christ . . .' (1 Peter 1:18-21)."* [DBS *Articles of Faith*, Section II, paragraph E, p. 5]

CHAPTER VI
AS DEAN BURGON, THE DEAN BURGON SOCIETY IS AN UNDAUNTED SOCIETY

A. Dean Burgon Was An UNDAUNTED Individual.

1. Burgon was UNDAUNTED In His Efforts To Defeat The "English Revised Version." As soon as the English Revised Version (ERV) appeared upon the scene in England in 1881, Dean Burgon wrote three articles on the faults and failures of it. All three articles later appeared in his book, *The Revision Revised,* published in 1883 which is available as **#611** for a GIFT of **$25.00+S&H**. It is 640 pages in length. It is a masterpiece which defends the King James Bible and demolishes the English Revised Version of 1881.

2. Burgon was UNDAUNTED In His Efforts To Defeat Westcott and Hort's Greek Text. Two of the sections in Burgon's *Revision Revised* dealt with the Westcott and Hort Greek text of the New Testament. One took up the deficiencies of the **theory** behind the Greek text. The other dismantled the Greek **text** itself, showing how it was wholly inadequate. In fact, he said it was the worst Greek text ever to see the light of day!

3. Burgon was UNDAUNTED In His Efforts To Defend The Very Words Of God. Burgon's defense of the very Words of God is no more evident than in his book, *Inspiration and Interpretation* (**#1220** for a GIFT of **$25.00+S&H**). Bear in mind what I mentioned on page 11:

*"Before looking at this section of quotations from Dean Burgon, it must be made clear that when he uses the word, "Bible," or "Holy Scripture," he is referring to the Hebrew/Aramaic and Greek **books, chapters, verses, words, letters, syllables, jots, and tittles** that God breathed out by inspiration and the various human writers wrote down as they were led by the Holy Spirit. Unless he makes it clear by the context, he does not refer to any **translation** of that "Bible," whether English, Spanish, French, German, or any other language. You should not be confused on this point. Dean Burgon has been misunderstood and misquoted in this very crucial point. Remember, unless otherwise defined, each time Dean Burgon uses the word,*

"Bible" or "Holy Scripture," he is referring to the original languages of Hebrew/Aramaic and Greek."

Listen to what Dean Burgon wrote:

"But if, instead of the 'theory of verbal inspiration,' I am asked whether I believe the words of the Bible to be inspired,--I answer, To be sure I do,--every one of them: and every syllable likewise: Do not you?--Where,--do you, in your wisdom, stop? The book, you allow is inspired. How about the chapters? How about the verses? Do you stop at the verses, and not go on to the words?" [Burgon, *Inspiration and Interpretation*, p. 751.

Hear him again:

"The Bible (be persuaded) Is the very utterance of the Eternal:--as much God's Word as if high heaven were open and heard God speaking to us with human voice. Every book of it, is inspired alike; and is inspired entirely. . . . But the Bible, from the Alpha to the Omega of it, is filled to overflowing with the Holy Spirit of God: the books of it, and the sentences of it, and the words of it, and the syllables of it.--aye, and the very letters of it." [Burgon, *Inspiration and Interpretation*, p. 6]

These two quotations, together with the many more in his book, show clearly Burgon's defense of the very Words of God, yea, even to the very syllables and letters of those words!

4. Burgon was UNDAUNTED In Study And Written Ministry. Burgon's entire adult life was spent in study and in written ministry. Though he was the author of dozens of books on other themes, consider the titles he penned on the subject of the Bible:(1) *The Last Twelve Verses of Mark* (#1139 for a gift of **$15.00+S&H**); (2) *The Revision Revised* (**#611** for a gift of **$25.00+S&H**); (3) *The Traditional Text* (#1159 for a gift of **$16.00+S&H**); (4) *The Causes of Corruption* (#1160 for a gift of **$15.00+S&H**); and (5) *Inspiration and Interpretation* (#1220 for a gift of **$25.00+S&H**).

5. Burgon was UNDAUNTED In The Face of Criticism And Misunderstanding. Burgon was criticized and misunderstood on two grounds: (1) He was adamantly opposed to the theological apostasy and unbelief within the ranks of the Anglican Church of his day; and (2) He was just as much in opposition to the erroneous Greek text and theory promulgated by Bishop Brooke Foss Westcott and Professor Fenton John Anthony Hort. Though both of these battlegrounds called forth much hatred for Dean Burgon, he remained undaunted, choosing rather to give himself even more unreservedly in his stand for the truth wherever God had given it.

B. As Dean Burgon, the Dean Burgon Society is An

Chapter VI: Dean Burgon & DBS--Both Undaunted

UNDAUNTED Society.

1. As Dean Burgon, The DBS Is UNDAUNTED In Its Efforts To Defeat The English Revised Version And Similar False Versions. The Dean Burgon Society is undaunted in its exposure of the faults and failings of the English Revised Version of 1881 by its circulation (as of this date)of over 2,000 copies of Burgon's *The Revision Revised* (#611 for a GIFT of **$25.00+S&H**). In fact, 3,000 additional copies had to be printed to keep up with the demand. This 640-page book has one third of its content in pointing out the defects and deficiencies of the ERV of 1881. The DBS has done the same in pointing out the defects and deficiencies in the New King James Version (cf. **#1442** for a gift of **$10.00+S&H**); the New American Standard Version (cf. **#1494-P** for a gift of **$15.00+S&H**); and the New International Version (cf. **#1749-P**, for a gift of **$25.00+S&H**). These are lengthy computer print-out studies which point out instances of dynamic equivalence in these three popular versions. These amount to over 2,000 for the NKJV, over 4,000 for the NASV, and over 6,653 for the NIV. There are scores of smaller tracts, pamphlets, tapes, and VCR's which also seek to defeat such perversions of God's original Words.

2. As Dean Burgon, the Dean Burgon Society Is UNDAUNTED In Its Efforts To Defeat Westcott and Hort's Greek Text. The Dean Burgon Society has exposed the Westcott and Hort false Greek Text by its circulation of Dean Burgon's *The Revision Revised* and his other books as mentioned above. There are also many other books, pamphlets, tracts, tapes, and VCR's which do the same. We have a **Brochure #1** which lists over 1,000 titles which in one way or another defend the King James Bible and its underlying Hebrew and Greek Texts and oppose the Westcott and Hort false Greek text.

3. As Dean Burgon, The DBS Is UNDAUNTED In Its Efforts To Defend the very Words of God. The Dean Burgon Society, in its *Articles of Faith*, in its publication the *DBS News*, and in its circulation of various materials, defends the very Words of God which we believe are best preserved in the Traditional Masoretic Hebrew Text and the Traditional Received Greek Text that underlie the King James Bible. We believe these are the very Words of God that have been providentially preserved for us from which our KJB was accurately translated by able translators using proper translation techniques.

4. As Dean Burgon, The DBS Is UNDAUNTED In Its Efforts To Study And Maintain A Written Ministry. The Dean Burgon Society believes in study. They also believe in having a written ministry through the *DBS News* and the other pamphlets and studies compiled by men on its Executive Committee and others. Each year, the VCR's, audio cassettes, and Message Books are made of the DBS Annual Meeting for use and edification of all who write for them.

5. As Dean Burgon, The DBS Is UNDAUNTED In Its Efforts In The Face Of Criticism And Misunderstanding. The Dean Burgon Society has had its share (and will continue to have its share) of both criticism and "misunderstanding." We go on, despite such things in an undaunted, victorious spirit, believing firmly that our cause is right, just, necessary, and proper. We will not give ground, nor give up our convictions!

CHAPTER VII
AS DEAN BURGON, THE DEAN BURGON SOCIETY IS A RELEVANT SOCIETY

A. Dean Burgon Was RELEVANT As An Individual.

1. Burgon was RELEVANT In Defending Bible Truth Against Error And Heresy. Dean Burgon shows his relevance in defending Bible truth against error and heresy in the way he spoke out and put in writing his own sadness at the apostasy and false teachings of his own Anglican Church. He was not liked very much for doing it, but again and again he wrote books and booklets exposing in a relevant manner the very errors his own churchmen were promulgating.

2. Burgon was RELEVANT In Defending The King James Bible Against An Inferior Version. Dean Burgon defended the King James Bible solidly and at length against the then-popular English Revised Version of 1881. His *Revision Revised* is an example of the skill he demonstrated in this defense.

3. Burgon was RELEVANT In Defending The Masoretic Hebrew Text That Underlies The King James Bible. Dean Burgon cautioned against the *"incredible folly of tinkering the Hebrew Text."* [Goulburn, *Biography*, Vol. II, p. 241] He felt that the Hebrew Text which underlies the King James Bible was all right and should not be "tinkered" or changed! He hoped that the English Revised Version Old Testament had not done that. If it had, it would have been *"incredible folly"*!

4. Burgon was RELEVANT In Defending The Traditional & Received Greek Text. Dean Burgon's five books (referred to above) are real examples of his relevant defense of the Traditional and Received Greek Text of the New Testament. Our #804 *(Dean Burgon's Warnings on Revision* for $7.00+S&H) is a study of Burgon's defense of this text, telling under what circumstances he would change the Greek and/or the King James Bible. The study takes quotations from Burgon's *Revision Revised* that pertain to the subject. Dean Burgon spent his entire adult life in the defense of what he termed "the Traditional Text" of the New Testament.

B. As Dean Burgon, the Dean Burgon Society Is A

RELEVANT Society.

1. As Dean Burgon, The DBS Is RELEVANT In Defending Bible Truth Against Error And Heresy. Though the Dean Burgon Society is a one-issue society, which is in defense of Traditional Bible Texts, we also have a sound and fundamental doctrinal statement which we will continue to defend. Since our doctrines include such things as the Trinity, the Person of Christ, the virgin birth of Christ, the bodily resurrection of Christ, salvation by grace through faith alone, a literal heaven and hell, spiritual unity of those redeemed "by His precious blood," the purity of the church, separation from unbelievers and disorderly believers, and a literal six-solar day creation by God of the entire world, the Dean Burgon Society defends aspects of these truths against any error or heresy.

2. As DEAN BURGON, The DBS Is RELEVANT In Defending The King James Bible Against Inferior Versions.
The 5th purpose of the Dean Burgon Society is:
> "*5. To defend the Traditional English Translation of the Bible--the King James Version (or Authorized Version)--as a true, faithful, and accurate translation from the underlying original texts which have been providentially preserved for us, which Translation has no equal in our time among all of the other English 'Translations.'*" [DBS *Articles of Faith*, III, B, 5, p. 71.

The 6th purpose of the Dean Burgon Society is:
> "*6. To expose and publicize the defects, deficiencies, errors, and mistakes both in the texts used and in the translation process and results of any and all modern translations of the Bible, whether in English, or in other languages, which are not based on the Traditional Masoretic Hebrew Text and Traditional Received Greek Text which underlie the King James Version.*" [DBS *Articles of Faith*, III, B, 6, p. 7]

This object has been fulfilled in the various materials, both written and spoken, circulated by the DBS.

3. As Dean Burgon, The DBS Is RELEVANT In Defending The Masoretic Hebrew Text. The 3rd purpose of the Dean Burgon Society is:
> "*3. To defend the Traditional Masoretic Hebrew Text of the Old Testament which underlies the King James Version.*" [DBS *Articles of Faith*, III, B, 3, p. 7]

Again, this object has been fulfilled in the various materials, both written and spoken circulated by the DBS.

4. As Dean Burgon, the DBS Is RELEVANT In Defending the Traditional And Received Greek Text. The 4th

Chapter VII: Dean Burgon & DBS—Both Relevant 41

purpose of the Dean Burgon Society is:

"4. To defend the Traditional Received Greek Text of the New Testament which underlies the King James Version (as found in 'The Greek Text Underlying The English Authorized Version of 1611 as published by the Trinitarian Bible Society in 1976')." [DBS Articles of Faith, III, B, 4, p. 71

Again, this object has been fulfilled in the various materials, both written and spoken circulated by the DBS.

CHAPTER VIII
AS DEAN BURGON, THE DEAN BURGON SOCIETY IS A GROWING SOCIETY

A. Dean Burgon Was a GROWING Individual.
   1. Burgon Was GROWING In the Knowledge Of the Scripture. Dean Burgon's studies in the New Testament Text showed him to be indeed **GROWING** in his knowledge of the Scripture. He wrote a commentary (which we have available) on each of the four Gospels. He studied the Word of God daily in order to be more knowledgeable in it. He recommended to his students who were going to be ministers to read through the Bible from Genesis to Revelation, spending one-half hour daily in this task.
   2. Burgon Was GROWING in the Understanding Of the Scripture. Not only did Dean Burgon **GROW** in "knowledge," but also in the "understanding" of the Scripture, depending, not on commentaries, or the words of men, but on the Holy Spirit to teach him.
   3. Burgon Was GROWING in Encouraging Others to Follow Him in His Use of Scripture. In the very first sermon to the preacher-boys of his day, Dean Burgon delivered a sermon entitled: "The Study of the Bible Recommended; and a Method of Studying it Described." From his sermon, as found in *Inspiration and Interpretation*, (available for a gift to DBS of **$25.00+S&H**), here are some quotations:
   "4. Then, while you read,--safe from the risk of interruption, (as I began by supposing,) and with every faculty intent on your task,--try, as much as possible, to go over the words as if they were new to you; and watch them, one by one, so that nothing may by any possibility escape your notice. Do not slumber over a single word. Nothing can be unimportant when it is the Holy Ghost who speaketh. It is an excellent practice to mark the expressions which strike you; for it is a method of preserving the memory of what is sure else soon to pass away." [Burgon, *Inspiration and Interpretation*, p. 10]
   "5. And next, be persuaded to read without extraneous helps of any kind; except, of course, such help as a map, or the margin of your Bible, supplies. Pray avoid Commentaries and notes. First, you cannot afford time for them: and secondly, if you could, they

Chapter VIII: Dean Burgon & DBS--Both Growing 43

would be as likely to mislead you as not. But the real reason why you are so strenuously advised to avoid them, is, because they will do more to nullify your reading, than anything which would be imagined. Your object is to obtain an insight into Holy Scripture, by acquiring the habit of reading it with intelligence and care; not to be saved trouble, and to be shown what other persons have thought about it." [Burgon, *Inspiration and Interpretation*, pp. 10-11] Many more quotations could be cited in this same sermon to this effect.

B. As Dean Burgon. The Dean Burgon Society Is A GROWING Society.

1. As Dean Burgon, The DBS Is GROWING In The Knowledge Of The Scripture. The Dean Burgon Society encourages its members and friends to continue in the study of the Word of God to obtain "knowledge" of what that Word contains.

2. As Dean Burgon, The DBS Is GROWING In The Understanding Of The Scripture. In addition, the Dean Burgon Society wants its members and friends to have a deeper "understanding" of the Bible. This is why they continue to publish the various papers, materials, books, tapes, and VCR's on Bible subjects.

3. As Dean Burgon, The DBS Is GROWING In Their Encouraging Of Others To Follow Their Position. The Dean Burgon Society has sought to be an encouragement to various groups to follow their position, such as the Awana International, the Trinitarian Bible Society, and the Majority Text Society. Comments have been made about these various groups both in the DBS pamphlets, the DBS annual meeting tapes, VCR's, DBS Message Books, and in the *Dean Burgon News*. We have even placed ads in the *Sword of the Lord* magazine in an effort to warn people about the Awana's change of their position regarding the exclusive use of the King James Bible in their programs and writings.

CHAPTER IX
AS DEAN BURGON, THE DEAN BURGON SOCIETY IS AN OBEDIENT SOCIETY

A. Dean Burgon Was an OBEDIENT Individual.
   1. Burgon was OBEDIENT In Exposing Error. Here are a few quotations about Dean John William Burgon's **OBEDIENCE** in exposing error of all sorts.
   a. Burgon Was Like A "Splendid Watch-dog." Goulburn wrote:
   "'What a splendid watch-dog he is!' said one in the author's hearing, after perusing and throwing on the table one of the Burgonian Philippics,--'How loud and furiously he barks, when the smallest danger threatens the Church, or the Faith which is entrusted to the Church's keeping!' Yes! It is the business of a watch-dog to bark furiously, and even to fly at the throat of pilferers and thieves: and of all pilferers and thieves there are none who more rouse the indignation of honest God-fearing men, than those who would rob the Church of her Faith, and the Christian of his hope, by the gradual depredations of rationalism." [Goulburn, *Biography*, Vol. II, p. 67]
   b. Burgon Admitted He Defended Strenuously When The "Words of Inspiration Are Seriously Imperilled." Burgon wrote:
   "If therefore, any do complain that I have sometimes hit my opponents rather hard, I take leave to point out that 'to everything there is a season, and a time to every purpose under the sun'; 'a time to embrace, and a time to be far from embracing'; a time for speaking smoothly, and a time for speaking sharply. And that when the words of inspiration are imperilled, as now they are, it is scarcely possible for one who is determined effectually to preserve the Deposit in its integrity, to hit either too straight or too hard." [Burgon, *The Revision Revised*, pp. vii-viii]
   c. Burgon "Thwarted," by His "Conservatism," the "Liberal Party" At Oxford More Than Once. Goulburn wrote:
   ". . . by a few disparaging words in Parliament, inspired no doubt

Chapter IX: Dean Burgon & DBS—Both Obedient

by the so-called liberal party in the University [that is, Oxford], who had been thwarted on more than one occasion by Burgon's stedfast and unflinching conservatism." [Goulburn, Biography, Vol. II, p. 136]

    d. Burgon Labeled "Disbelief in the Bible as the Word of God" as the "Fundamental Error." Burgon wrote:

"At the root of the whole mischief of these last days lies disbelief in the Bible as the Word of God. This is the fundamental error." [Burgon, Inspiration and Interpretation, p. xvii]

    e. Burgon Wanted to "Defend" the Bible "Without Compromise." He wrote:

". . . we are constrained to give a reason for the hope which is in us; and to defend without compromise or hesitation that Bible which is the great bulwark of the Faith." [Burgon, Inspiration and Interpretation, p. 12]

    f. Burgon Was "Jealous" for the "Honour of the Lord." He wrote:

"Be as forgiving as you please of indignities offered to yourselves; but do not be ashamed to be very jealous for the honour of the Lord of Hosts; and to resent any dishonour offered to Him, with a fiery indignation utterly unlike anything you could possibly feel for a personal wrong." [Burgon, Inspiration and Interpretation, p. 121]

    g. Burgon Exposed the Heresies of "Six Ministers of the Church of England" in Their *Essays and Reviews.*"

    (1) The "*Essays and Reviews*" Denied The Fundamentals Of The Faith. Burgon wrote:

"Secondly,--'Essays and Reviews' attracted notice because six of its authors were ministers of the Church of England. Here were six clergymen openly making light of their sacred profession. . . . As an infidel, but certainly in this instance most truthful as well as an able Reviewer, remarked concerning the work in question,--'In their ordinary, if not plain sense, there has been discarded the Word of God, the creation, the fall, the redemption, justification, heaven and hell, eternal punishment and a day of judgment, creeds, liturgies, and articles, the truth of Jewish history and of Gospel narrative, a sense of doubt thrown over even the incarnation, the resurrection, and ascension, the Divinity of the Second Person, and the Personality of the Third.'" [Burgon, Inspiration, and Interpretation, p. xi]

    (2) Burgon Treated the "Six Clergymen" as "Immoral Characters." He wrote:

"When Critics are clamorous for the 'free handling' of Divine Truth, they must not be surprised to find themselves freely handled too . .

...*six clergymen of the Church of England who enter upon a crusade against the Faith of the Church of England must not be astonished if they are looked upon in the light of immoral characters, and treated as such. Accordingly, I have handled them just as freely as they have handled the Prophets, Apostles, and Evangelists of Christ."* [Burgon, Inspiration and Interpretation, p. xxvi]

(3) Burgon Did Not Expect "Blasphemy from Ministers of the Gospel." He wrote:

"Some respectable persons, I doubt not, will think my treatment of them harsh and uncharitable. I invite them to consider that we do not expect blasphemy from ministers of the Gospel,--irreligion from the teachers of youth,--infidelity from the professor's chair: nor are we called upon to tolerate it either." [Burgon, Inspiration and Interpretation, p. xxiv]

(4) Burgon Denounced "Uncompromisingly" this "Volume" Which Was to "Sap the Foundation of Faith." He wrote:

". . . 'Essays and Reviews' . . . a volume, the confessed tendency of which is to sap the foundation of faith and to introduce irreligion with a flood-tide. . . . their Reviewer [Burgon himself] *avails himself of that Christian liberty to which they themselves so systematically lay claim, mercilessly to uncover their baseness and uncompromisingly to denounce it. If I may declare my mind freely, punctilious courtesy in dealing with such opinions, becomes a species of treason against him after whose Name we are called, and whom we profess to serve. Seven men may combine to handle the things of God; it seems, in the most outrageous manner; while themselves are to be the objects of consideration, tenderness, respect! I cannot see their title to any consideration at all."* [Burgon, Inspiration and Interpretation, p. xxiv]

(5) Burgon Gave an Example of Their Method of Believing Doctrine "Only Ideologically True Yet Historically False." He wrote:

"We are assured that every one of these things, are only ideologically true that [the doctrines of the Faith, or at least some of them], *historically they are false. . . . I therefore proceed to give you a sample of this kind of teaching. A living dignitary of our Church writes as follows concerning the transfiguration of Christ. 'It may be asked, of what kind was the vision which we here call the Transfiguration? Was it an effect produced within on the minds of the Apostles; or was it that an actual external change came for the time over the person of our Lord? We cannot say. I give you this as the mildest form of the poison. Quite evident is it that the same suggestion is just as applicable to our Lord's Birth, or to His Death;*

Chapter IX: Dean Burgon & DBS--Both Obedient 47

to His Temptation, or to His Resurrection." [Burgon, *Inspiration and Interpretation*, pp. 244-45]

(6) Burgon Held up to "Ridicule" and "Unqualified Reprobation" Those Ministers Who Put Forth Such "Blasphemous Folly." He wrote:

"Not only will I not treat men with tenderness who put forth such blasphemous folly, but I will hold them up to the very utmost of my power. Nay, I would make them objects of unqualified reprobation to all, if I could, as they deserve to be reprobated; for they are the worst enemies of the Gospel of Christ." [Burgon, *Inspiration and Interpretation*, pp. 248-49]

In a footnote after writing this statement, Burgon wrote a comment:

"I have softened the expression originally employed in this place, out of deference to the opinions of some wise and good men. But I do not think that St. John (the Evangelist and Apostle of dogma,) would have thought my language too strong: nor St. Paul either." [Burgon, *Inspiration and Interpretation*, pp. 248-49]

(7) Burgon Called on the Heretical "Essayists and Reviewers" to "Resign Their Stations" in the Church. He wrote:

"They [that is, the Essayists and Reviewers] *must first withdraw from the cause which they have betrayed; cease to profess the teaching which they disbelieve; resign their commission in a Church to whose doctrine and discipline they openly proclaim themselves to be opposed. I will not argue with them, while they presume to write B.D. and D.D. after their names,--hold Chaplaincies,--preside over Schools and Colleges,--profess to lecture in Divinity,--officiate at the altars of the Church of England,--by virtue of their sacred office, and by virtue of that only, are instructors of youth. They cannot, (if they are in the full enjoyment of their faculties,) cannot imagine, for a moment, that, as honest men, they can remain where they are! They must either recall their words or resign their stations!"* [Burgon, *Inspiration and Interpretation*, p, xxviii]

From the above quotations, there certainly can be no doubt whatever about Dean John William Burgon's absolute obedience in exposing error even right within his own Church of England! He was a man of courage, unwilling to keep quiet for the sake of personal advantage, but exposing heresy wherever he found it--even when it was in his own Church family! I wish more men would follow his courage today within their own churches where compromise and apostasy's influence abounds!

2. Burgon was OBEDIENT In Defending The Bible.

The following are some of the many quotations that could be brought forward showing Dean Burgon's **OBEDIENCE** in defending the Bible.

a. Burgon Thought You Should Believe "The Whole

of Holy Scripture" or "Disbelieve the Whole." He wrote:
"Either, with the best and wisest of all ages, you must believe the whole of Holy Scripture; or, with the narrow-minded infidel, you must disbelieve the whole. There is no middle course open to you." [Burgon, *Inspiration and Interpretation*, p. 46]

      b. Burgon Had Some Suggestions For Bible Reading And Bible Study For His Students Entering The Ministry.

         (1) **The Bible Should Be His Students' Only Textbook For Three Years.** He wrote:
"Be content, for the next three years to study no book of Divinity but the Bible." [Burgon, *Inspiration and Interpretation*, p. 29]

         (2) **His Students Should Read the "Whole Bible Consecutively Through."** He wrote:
"The thing I would so strenuously urge upon you, is--that, during your undergraduate period, you should read the whole Bible consecutively through. from one end to the other, by yourself and for yourself, with consummate method, care, and attention." [Burgon, *Inspiration and Interpretation*, p. 9]

         (3) **His Students Should Spend the "Quietest Half-hour in the Whole Day" for Bible Reading.** He wrote
"1. First, that you should deliberately apportion to this solemn duty the best and freshest and quietest half-hour in the whole day; and then, that you should determine, let what will go undone, never to abridge that half-hour." [Burgon, *Inspiration and Interpretation*, p. 9]

         (4) **Bible Reading Should Be "Strictly Consecutive."** He wrote:
"6. Above all, is it indispensable that your reading of the Bible should be strictly consecutive; and on no account may any one pretend to begin such a study of that book as I am here recommending, except at the first chapter of Genesis." [Burgon, *Inspiration and Interpretation*, p. 11]

         (5) **No Book Or Chapter Should Be "Skipped."** He wrote:
"7. It will follow from what has been offered, that you are invited to read every book in the Bible in the order in which it actually stands-- never of course skipping a chapter much less a book: in every mere catalogue of names, be resolved to find edification. Feel persuaded that details, seemingly the driest, are full of God." [Burgon, *Inspiration and Interpretation*, p. 12]

      c. Burgon Gave Repeated Testimony To His Belief In And Defense Of The Bible's Inspiration, Inerrancy, And Perfection. Here again, bear in mind what I wrote on pages 11 and 31:

Chapter IX: Dean Burgon & DBS--Both Obedient 49

*"Before looking at this section of quotations from Dean Burgon, it must be made clear that when he uses the word, "**Bible**," or "**Holy Scripture**," he is referring to the Hebrew/Aramaic and Greek **books, chapters, verses, words, letters, syllables, jots, and tittles** that God breathed out by inspiration and the various human writers wrote down as they were led by the Holy Spirit. **Unless he makes it clear by the context**, he does not refer to any **translation** of that "**Bible**," whether English, Spanish, French, German, or any other language. You should not be confused on this point. Dean Burgon has been misunderstood and misquoted in this very crucial point. Remember, unless otherwise defined, each time Dean Burgon uses the word, "**Bible**" or "**Holy Scripture**," he is referring to the original languages of Hebrew/Aramaic and Greek."*

(1) Burgon Believed the Bible Is a "Direct Message from the Presence-Chamber of the Lord of Heaven and Earth." He wrote::
"Theological Science not so! Her evidence is sure, for her Rule is God's Word. No laborious induction here,--fallacious because imperfect; imperfect because human: but a direct message from the Presence-Chamber of the Lord of heaven and earth,--decisive because inspired; infallible because Divine. The express Revelation of the Eternal is that whereon theological Science builds her fabric of imperishable Truth; that fabric which, while other modes change, shift, and at last become superseded, shines out,--yea, and to the very end of time will shine out,--unconscious of decay, incapable of improvement, far, far beyond fashion: a thing unchanged, because in its very nature unchangeable." [Burgon, *Inspiration and Interpretation*, p. 50]

(2) Burgon Held "Verbal Inspiration" to Be a Fact, Not Merely a "Theory." He wrote:
"Do you mean to say then, (I shall be asked,) that you maintain the theory of verbal inspiration?--I answer, I refuse to accept any theory whatsoever. But I believe that the Bible is the Word of God--and I believe that God's Word must be absolutely infallible. I shall therefore believe the Bible to be absolutely infallible,--until I am convinced of the contrary." [Burgon, *Inspiration and Interpretation*, p. 74]
Burgon added:
"But if, instead of the 'theory of verbal inspiration' I am asked whether I believe the Words of the Bible to be inspired,--I answer, to be sure I do--every one of them: and every syllable. Do not you?--where,--(if it be a fair question,)--where do you, in your wisdom, stop? The book, you allow, is inspired. How about the chapters? How about the verses? Do you stop at the verses, and

not go on to the words?" [Burgon, *Inspiration and Interpretation*, p. 75].

(3) **Burgon Believed Even the Very "Letters" of the Bible Were "Inspired."** He wrote:

"The Bible (be persuaded) is the very utterance of the Eternal:--as much God's Word as if high heaven were open, and we heard God speaking to us with human voice. Every book of it is inspired alike: and is inspired entirely . . . . but the Bible, from the Alpha to the Omega of it, is filled to overflowing with the Holy Spirit of God: the books of it, and the sentences of it, and the words of it, and the syllables of it,--aye, and the very letters of it." [Burgon, *Inspiration and Interpretation*, p. 76]

(4) **Burgon Believed The Entire Bible To Be From God Himself And Vitally Important.**

(a) Burgon Believed That Every "WORD" Is Important. He wrote:

"Do not slumber over a single word. Nothing can be unimportant when it is the Holy Ghost who speaketh." [Burgon, *Inspiration and Interpretation*, p. 19]

(b) Burgon Believed Literally The Genesis Creation. He wrote:

"He who surrenders the first page of his Bible surrenders all. He knows not where to stop." [Burgon, *Inspiration and Interpretation*, p. 50]

(c) Burgon Believed Every Single "Letter" of the Bible Is the "Voice of Him That Sitteth upon the Throne." He wrote:

". . .The Bible is none other than the voice of Him that sitteth upon the throne! Every book of it,--every chapter of it,--every verse of it,--every word of it,--every syllable of it,--(where do we stop?) every letter of it--is the direct utterance of the Most High!--<u>pasa graphE theopneustos</u>. Well spake the Holy Ghost, by the mouth of the many blessed men who wrote it.--The Bible is none other than the Word of God: not some part of it, more, some part of it, less; but all alike, the utterance of Him who sitteth upon the throne:--absolute,--faultless,--unerring,--supreme!" [Burgon, *Inspiration and Interpretation*, p. 89]

(d) Burgon Repeated Again His Confidence in the Very "Words" of God as If "God Spoke to Us Therein with Human Lips." He wrote:

"Some here present may remember my repeated and unequivocal

assertion that Holy Scripture is inspired from the Alpha to the Omega of it:--not some parts of it more, some parts less. But all equally, and all to overflowing:--that we hold it to be, not generally inspired, but particularly; that we see not how with logical consistency we can avoid believing the words as well as the sentences of it; the syllables as well as words; the letters as well as the syllables; every 'jot' and every 'tittle' of it, (to use our Lord's expression,) to be Divinely inspired:--and further, that until the contrary has been proven, we shall maintain that no misapprehension or misstatement, no error or blot of any kind, can possibly exist within its pages:--that we hold the Bible to be as much the Word of God, as if God spoke to us therein with human lips:--and that, as the very utterance of the Holy Ghost, we cannot but think that it must be absolute, faultless, unerring, supreme." [Burgon, *Inspiration and Interpretation*, p. 94]

(e) Burgon Held The Bible To Be "THE VERY UTTERANCE OF THE HOLY SPIRIT." He wrote:

". . . when we call the Bible an inspired book, we mean nothing more than that the words of it are the very utterance of the Holy Spirit:--that the book is as much the Word of God as if high heaven were open, and we heard God speaking to us with human voice." [Burgon, *Inspiration and Interpretation*, p. 102]

(f) Burgon Believed a Person Should "Read" the Bible, Believing It Is an "Inspired Book." He wrote:

". . . I say, that they [that is, the "younger men present"] would now be assiduous, and earnest, and regular, and punctual, and devout, in their daily study of one chapter of the Bible.--And while you read the Bible, read it believing that you are reading an inspired Book:--not a Book inspired in parts only, but a Book inspired in every part:--not a Book unequally inspired, but all inspired equally:--not a Book generally inspired,--the substance indeed given by the Spirit, but the words left to the option of the writers; but the words of it as well as the matter of it, all--all given by God. As it is written--'Man shall not live by bread alone, but by every word that proceedeth out of the mouth of God.'" [Burgon, *Inspiration and Interpretation*, p. 114]

(g) Burgon Didn't Believe You Could "Expound a Text" Unless You Believe its "Words Are Inspired." He wrote:

"How can you pretend to expound a text, unless you hold the words of that text to be inspired? What inferences can you venture to draw from words, the Divinity of which you dare not affirm?" [Burgon,

Inspiration and Interpretation, p. 117]

(h) Burgon Had a Burden and Passed it on to His Ministerial Students to "Preserve the Whole Deposit of Heaven-Descended Teaching." He wrote:

"O let it be our great concern,--yours and mine,--to preserve with undiminished lustre the whole Deposit of heaven-descended teaching which is the Church's treasure. Like runners in a certain ancient race of which we all have read, let it be our pride and joy,-- yours and mine,--to grasp the torch of Truth with a strong unwavering hand; to run joyously with it so long as the days of this earthly race shall last; and dying, to hand it to another, who, with strength renewed like the eagle's, may again,--swiftly, steadily, exultingly,--run with it, till he fails! . . . so, when the Judge of quick and dead appeareth,--so let Him find you occupied, . . ." [Burgon, *Inspiration and Interpretation*, p. 180]

(i) Burgon Believed the Bible to Be a "Celestial Armoury" Which Contains a "Weapon Against Every Foe." He wrote:

"Begin betimes to acquaint yourselves with the wealth of that celestial armoury which contains a weapon which must prove fatal to every foe; but which it depends on yourselves whether you shall have the skill to wield or not. Suffer not yourselves to be cheated of your birthright, the Bible, either by the novel fictions of unstable men, or by the exploded heresies of a bygone age, revived and recommended by living unbelievers. You, especially, who aspire to the Ministerial office, and are destined hereafter to undertake the cure of souls, O do you be doubly watchful! Give to the Bible the undivided homage of a childlike heart; and bow down before its revelations with a supliant understanding also; and let no characteristic of its method by any means escape you." [Burgon, *Inspiration and Interpretation*, p. 253]

From these quotations, you can see clearly just how Dean John William Burgon was obedient in **DEFENDING** the Bible! I wish that every born again Christian living today would have as high a view of the Bible as did Dean Burgon!

3. Burgon was OBEDIENT In "Declaring Bible Truths." Dean Burgon preached each week, proclaiming and declaring Bible truths. He had a special Bible study class for some of his students which also occupied him in the ministry. In his various books, especially in his exposition of the Four Gospels, Burgon was **OBEDIENT** in declaring the various Bible truths found therein.

Chapter IX: Dean Burgon & DBS--Both Obedient

B. As Dean Burgon, the Dean Burgon Society Is an OBEDIENT Society.

1. As Dean Burgon, The DBS Is OBEDIENT In Exposing Error And Heresy. The Dean Burgon Society exposes error and heresy, especially as it concerns the Bible. Its doctrinal statement covers many areas of Bible truth. Where these Bible truths are transgressed, the DBS exposes such error.

2. As Dean Burgon, The DBS Is OBEDIENT In Defending The Bible. We recognize that in these days, the Bible is under severe and determined attack. Throughout its *Articles of Faith*, the Dean Burgon Society has taken bold positions in its defense of the Bible. Its motto is "In Defense of Traditional Bible Texts." It will continue to defend the King James Bible as the "Word of God in English," and the original-language texts of Hebrew and Greek on which it is based. In addition, it will defend all of the Bible doctrines contained therein, seeking to repel any and all attacks thereto.

3. As DEAN BURGON, The DBS Is OBEDIENT In Declaring Bible Truths. Again, the Dean Burgon Society declares Bible truths to the extent of its own doctrinal statement and beliefs, though its primary purpose is the declaration of truths relating to the Bible itself, "In Defense of Traditional Bible Texts."

CHAPTER X
AS DEAN BURGON, THE DEAN BURGON SOCIETY IS A NEEDED SOCIETY

A. Dean Burgon Was a NEEDED Individual.

1. Burgon was NEEDED To Write Books And Materials. Dean Burgon, as mentioned above, was a prolific writer! His books dealing with the Scripture text alone are five in number, with a total of almost 2,000 pages "In Defense of Traditional Bible Texts." Though he had enemies, yet his books and materials were definitely needed. They are still needed today as well.

2. Burgon was NEEDED To Combat False Teaching. With his Anglican Church moving rapidly into Catholicism and Apostasy, Dean Burgon's voice was needed to combat this false teaching. Again, though his Church did not appreciate his voice, like that of a "watch dog," he was nonetheless **NEEDED** in that arena.

3. Burgon was NEEDED To Combat A False Basis Of Determining The Greek Text. Dean Burgon was a trained Greek scholar. He was familiar with the sources of the Greek New Testament. When the Traditional Greek Text was under assault by Westcott and Hort and their followers, Burgon raised his voice and his pen to combat this false basis of determining the Greek text which was used by this team of textual traitors!

4. Burgon was NEEDED To Get Out His Distinctive Message. Amidst the loud and lofty voices clamoring for a hearing in the area of the Greek New Testament, Dean Burgon was needed to get out his distinctive message in support of the "Traditional Text" of the New Testament. He knew that there must be a consideration of all of the evidence, and not merely a brief look at the Vatican ("B") and/or the Sinai ("Aleph") manuscripts. He held that these manuscripts are the most foul sources that ever saw the light of day. Burgon proved this to the satisfaction of any objective reader in his five books referred to above. It was of the utmost importance that the false teaching of Westcott and Hort with their new and perverted Greek Text of the New Testament should be answered right from their own Church and in their own time. This is what makes it so important for us today to read Dean Burgon's materials carefully. It helps us in the battle today because the

Chapter X: Dean Burgon & DBS--Both Needed 55

same false theories are still with us.

B. As DEAN BURGON, The DEAN BURGON SOCIETY Is A NEEDED Society.

1. As Dean Burgon, The DBS Is NEEDED To Write Books And Materials. The printed page is very powerful since it has a lasting effect on its readers. Tapes and VCR's are good, and the Dean Burgon Society uses them, but our pamphlets, papers, the *Dean Burgon News*, and books which we circulate are very much **NEEDED** in this lop-sided presentation of the entire truth concerning the New Testament text. Almost all of the major publishers publish books that favor the Westcott & Hort side of this battle. DBS joins with the few other organizations that contribute needed books and other materials for the cause.

2. As DEAN BURGON, The DBS Is NEEDED To Combat False Teaching. The Dean Burgon Society fills a need in its combat with false teaching that is contrary to its *Articles of Faith*, and especially in the area of Bible texts and translations. We do not believe, for example, that the King James Bible is "God-breathed," "inspired by God" and a "Revelation from God" as were the original Hebrew/Aramaic and Greek texts. It is rather an accurate "translation." There is considerable error on this point which is being disseminated by Dr. Peter Ruckman and his followers. The DBS combats this "double inspiration" theory as it has been called.

3. As DEAN BURGON, The DBS Is NEEDED To Combat A False Basis Of Determining The Greek Text. The Dean Burgon Society circulates over 1,000 titles which combat the false basis of determining the Greek text such as taught by Westcott and Hort and their modern day followers. Through the printed page, audio and video cassettes, annual meetings, Bible seminars, and through their radio programs, they seek to combat and expose Westcott and Hortism in all of its modern garb. We feel that the so-called "Majority Text" of Hodges and Farstad is not the proper, Burgonian way of determining the Greek text of the New Testament, and we have several written materials as well as audio and video cassettes giving our reasons for this.

4. As Dean Burgon, The DBS Is NEEDED To Get Out Our Distinctive Message. There can be no question but that the Dcan Burgon Society is **NEEDED** in our days in order to get out our distinctive message favoring the Traditional Masoretic Hebrew Text and the Traditional Received Greek Text that underlie the King James Bible, as well as defending the King James Bible as being the only accurate and faithful English translation in existence today! We trust that the Lord will keep us in our firm and vigilant stance until He comes, and that our DBS Executive Committee and Advisory Council will continue to function and to be active in fulfillment of our objectives and purposes!

CONCLUDING REMARKS

In view of the foregoing pages, I want to leave you with these summary thoughts: (1) Keep being faithful to our cause! (2) Keep praying for our cause! (3) Keep giving to our cause!

And remember, the Dean Burgon Society is well deserving of its name, because:

1. **"D"**--As DEAN BURGON, The DBS is a **Defending** Society.

2. **"E"**--As DEAN BURGON, The DBS is an **Educational** Society.

3. **"A"**--As DEAN BURGON, The DBS is an **Adamant** Society.

4. **"N"**--As DEAN BURGON, The DBS is a **Neglected** Society.

5. **"B"**--As DEAN BURGON, The DBS is a **Believing** Society.

6. **"U"**--As DEAN BURGON, The DBS is an **Undaunted** Society.

7. **"R"**--As DEAN BURGON, The DBS is a **Relevant** Society.

8. **"G"**--As DEAN BURGON, The DBS is a **Growing** Society.

9. **"O"**--As DEAN BURGON, The DBS is an **Obedient** Society.

10. **"N"**--As DEAN BURGON, The DBS is a **Needed** Society.

Won't YOU pray about it, read our *Articles of Faith*, and, if you agree with our stand, **JOIN US IN OUR BATTLE FOR GODS TRUTH!**

Index of Words and Phrases

0% of the non-MSS evidence ... 9
1,000 titles .... xiv, 24, 37, 55
10% of the manuscript evidence . 8
10% of the MSS evidence 8
100 .... x, 7-10
100 of the ancient Lectionaries .. 7
100% 8-10
100% of the evidence 8-10
11 words 4
11% of all evidence 8
140,521 4
140,521 Greek words 4
1550 years old 5
1611 .... x, 10, 11, 21, 23, 33, 41
169 words 4
1850/5 vii
1850/VC2 vii
1873 .... xii, 18
1881 .... xiii, xv, 19, 20, 22
30, 35, 37, 39
1967 .... 8, 9
1967 totals 8, 9
1978 .... v, vii, 1, 23, 31
2,000 pages 54
20 .... xiii, 8, 9, 28
26th or 27th edition ..... x, 5, 7, 8
300 .... 8, 9
39 changes 4
39 words 4
500 more copies .... x, 6
7% of all evidence 9
8,765 4
8,765 Greek words 4
8% of the MSS evidence 9
801 pages 3
90% 4
99.6% accurate 4
99.9% accurate 4
abhor 17
absolute 13, 47, 50, 51
absolutely infallible 49
accurate translation 20, 22, 27
28, 40
acrostic .... vii, ix, 2
Adamant . vii, xiv, xv, 2, 25-27, 56
Aland .... x, 5-8
Aleph 54
all the verses 21, 27
all the verses in the King James
Version 21
Alpha to the Omega 12, 36, 50, 51
ancient Greek Fathers .... x, 7
ancient Lectionaries 7
ancient versions .... x, 7-10
Andrew Brown 10
Anglican bishop .... xv, 30
Anglican Church ... xi, 13, 17, 30
36, 39, 54
Anglicanism 1
Anglo-Saxon language . xi, 10, 11
Apocryphal Books .... xi, 12
apostasy . 13, 15, 27, 30, 36, 39, 54
apostles 3, 10, 16, 26, 32, 46
Articles of Faith .. xii, xiv, 1, 14,
20-24, 28, 29, 33, 34,37, 40
41, 53, 55, 56
ascension 15, 45
astray .... ix, 4, 5
atoning power 34
atoning power of His redeeming
blood 34
audio .... vii, xiv, 24, 37, 55
auricular confession 19
authenticity 3
authoritative ...... ix-xi, 6, 8, 11
authoritative revision ix-xi, 6, 8, 11
authoritative revisions x
Authorized Version 8, 9, 11, 20-22
28, 33, 40, 41
autographs 20, 27

Awana 24, 43	book of reference 11
Awana Churches 24	books of it 12, 36, 50
Awana's errors 24	brochure #1 37
B .... iv, ix-xx, 1-6, 10, 12, 14, 17	Brooke Foss Westcott 36
18, 20, 23-30, 33, 36, 39-41	Brown 10
43, 44, 47, 48, 50, 52, 54-56	Burgon .... 1, 3-v, vii, ix-xx
B.D. 18, 47	1-28, 30-56
bark furiously 14, 44	burning zeal .... xiv, 26
barked furiously .... xi, 13	burning zeal for God's truth ... 26
baseness 16, 46	Calvary Baptist Church vii
believe the whole 48	candles 19
Believing . vii, xv, xvi, xviii, xix, 2	*Causes of Corruption* 23, 36
12, 13, 32-34, 38, 46, 51, 56	celestial armoury .... xx, 52
best learning 6	champion .... xv, 26
betrayal 15	champion in a cause ...... xv, 26
Betrayal of a Sacred Trust 15	chapters 11, 12, 35, 36, 49
betrayed 17, 26, 47	chasuble 19
#1448 10	Chichester 1, 3
#1619 3	childlike heart 52
#1727 10	Church Fathers 8-10
#611 5	Church of England . xiii, xviii, 15,
#804 39	16, 18, 19, 45-47
Bible ...... v, x, xi, xiii-xx, 1, 5, 8	*Closer Look, A* 8, 9
10-13, 16, 19-24, 27, 28, 31-33,	collated .... x, 6, 7
35-37, 39-43, 45, 47-55	commentaries 42
Bible an inspired book 51	commentaries and notes 42
Bible For Today 24	commonly received text is
Bible Preservation 23	the true one 5
Biblical learning 6	communion .... xii, 18, 19
Biblical separation 27	companion .... xi, 11
Biography .. 3, 5, 14, 15, 17-20, 25	companion in the study .... xi, 11
26, 30, 32, 33, 39, 44, 45	compare Scripture with
birettas 19	Scripture 21, 33
blasphemous folly ... xviii, 17, 47	compromise .... xiv, xv, xviii
blasphemy ...... xii, xviii, 16, 46	25, 26, 45, 47
blood .... xvi, 27, 33, 34, 40	compromise was a word
blood and grace of our	unknown to him 25
Divine Lord 33	condemn it 17
blot .... xi, 13, 51	confession 19
book .... vii, xi, xix, 5, 6, 9, 11-13	conservatism ..... xii, xviii, 14, 45
15, 18, 19, 23, 24, 32	consummate ability and learning 11
35-37, 48-51,	controversial efforts 26
Book of Common Prayer .. 18, 19	controverted passages 11

Index of Words and Phrases

convinced himself 25
courage .... xiv, 25, 47
courtesy .... xii, 16, 46
creation ...... xv, xvi, xix, 15, 24
    27, 32, 33, 40, 45, 50
creeds 15, 45
critical edition of the N.T. 5
critical purposes 11
crusade against the faith ... 16, 46
cursives 8, 9
D.D..................... 47
danger .... xi, 13, 14, 28, 44
Darwinian theory 33
DBS .. v, xiii-xviii, xx, 1, 2, 20-24
    26, 27, 30, 31, 33, 34, 37
    38, 40-43, 53, 55, 56
DBS annual meeting 38, 43
DBS News 23, 37
Dean ..... 1, 3-v, vii, ix, xiii-xviii
    xx, 1-5, 8-14, 20-28
    30-44, 47, 49, 52-56
Dean Burgon .... 1, 3-v, vii, ix
    xiii-xviii, xx, 1-5, 9-12
    20-27, 30 44, 49, 52-56
Dean Burgon News 1, 23, 31
    43, 55
Dean Burgon Society 1, 3-v
    vii, ix, xiii-xviii, xx, 1-3, 5, 20,
    23-27, 30, 32, 33, 35-44, 52-56
*Dean Burgon's Warnings on
    Revision* 39
Dean John William
    Burgon .. 1, 3, vii, 10, 28, 52
Dean of Chichester 1, 3
*Defects in the New American
    Standard Version* 24
*Defects in the New International
    Version* 24
*Defects in the New King James
    Version* 23
defend without compromise ... 45
Defending .. vii, ix, xiii, xvii, xviii
    xx, 2, 3, 20, 24, 39, 40, 47,

    52, 53, 55, 56
defending society ...... ix, xiii, 2
    3, 20, 56
deficiencies . 21, 22, 28, 35, 37, 40
delivered himself with courage . 25
deposit .... xix, 14, 44, 52
de-Christianizing 15
difficult 11, 27
difficult and controverted
    passages 11
diligently collated .... x, 6
diligently inspecting .... x, 7
direct utterance of the Most
    High 50
disbelief in the Bible .... xviii, 45
disbelieve the whole .... xviii, 48
discarded the Word of God . 15, 45
Disestablishment of
    Religion .... xii, 15
Divine Master .... ix, 3
Divine truth .... xii, 15, 45
Divinely inspired 13, 51
Divines 6
Divinity 13, 15, 18, 19
    45, 47, 48, 51
doctrinal basis .... ix, 1
double inspiration 55
doubly watchful 52
Dr. Jack Moorman 8, 9
dying rather than recalling 25
Dynamic equivalence 37
E.R.V..................... 3
*Early Manuscripts and the
    Authorized Version* 8, 9
eastward position 19
edited afresh .... x, 7
Educational .... vii, xiii, xiv, 2
    23, 24, 56
educational tools 23
Edward Meyrick Goulburn 3
Edward Miller 4
eight 6
enemies of the gospel 17, 47

English divines 6
English New Testament .... xi, 11
English Revised Version . xiii, xv,
  xvi, 19, 22, 30,35, 37, 39
English Revised Version of
  1881 .. xiii, 19, 22, 35, 37, 39
Englishmen .... x, 6, 7
erred 6
error . xi, xii, xvii, xviii, xx, 13, 17
  19, 39, 40, 44, 45, 47, 51, 53, 55
ERV .... xv, 22, 30, 35, 37
Essays and Reviews ..... xii, xviii
  15, 16, 45
essentially the same 5
essentially the same in all 5
eternal punishment 15, 45
eternal Sonship 26
Eucharist 19
evangelists 10, 16, 26, 46
every book of it inspired alike . 12
every syllable ... xi, 12, 36, 49, 50
every word 13, 30, 50, 51
every 'jot' and every 'tittle' of it 13
evidence 7-10, 49, 54
evidence they afford 7
evolution 33
exactly collated .... x, 7
exactly eight 6
excellent text as it stands .. ix, 4, 5
expose 13, 21, 22, 28, 40, 55
extant 8, 9
facile princeps 6
faithful . 19, 20, 22, 28, 40, 55, 56
fall 15, 45
false principles 8, 9
false principles of Westcott
  and Hort 8, 9
false versions .... xvi, 37
Farstad .... x, 5, 6, 8, 9, 55
fasting 19
fatal to every foe 52
Fathers .... x, 7-10
faultless 13, 50, 51

feel sure of 25
Fellow of Oriel College 18
Fenton John Anthony Hort 36
fiery indignation 45
filled to overflowing ... 12, 36, 50
filled to overflowing with the Holy
  Spirit of God 12, 36, 50
florid ritual .... xii, 18
folly ...... ix, xviii, 3, 17, 39, 47
force of will .... xiv, 25
foundation of faith xii, xviii, 16, 46
founding 1, 23
fourteen requirements ...... ix, 5
freely handled 16, 45
from the Alpha to the Omega
  of it 12, 36, 50, 51
fundamentalist 27
fundamentalist society 27
future revision of the English 6, 11
generally inspired 12, 13, 51
Genesis to Revelation .. xv, 21, 32
  33, 42
genius .... x, 10, 26
giants 10
giants in those days 10
given by God 13, 51
good enough .... ix, 4, 5
good enough for all ordinary
  purposes .... ix, 4, 5
gospel narrative 15, 45
Goulburn . 3, 14, 17-19, 25, 26, 32
  33, 44
grace of our Divine Lord 33
grasp the torch of truth 52
Greek scholar 54
Griesbach 5
Growing .... vii, xvii, xviii, 2
  42, 43, 56
guardians 26
half-hour .... xix, 48
handmaid 11
hard-hitting terms 30
he stood and acted alone 25

Index of Words and Phrases

he who surrenders the first page 50
heaven .... xix, 12, 15, 24, 36, 40
    45, 49-52
heaven-descended teaching xix, 52
Hebrew .... ix, xiii, xvii, 3, 11, 12
    20-22, 24, 27, 28, 31, 35-37,
    39, 40, 49, 53, 55
Hebrew Text ix, xiii, xvii, 3, 20-22
    27, 28, 31, 37, 39, 40, 55
hell 15, 24, 40, 45
Hellenistic scholarship 6
heresy .... xi-xiii, xvii, xx, 13, 17
    21, 39, 40, 47, 53
heretics .... xii, 13, 17
high heaven were open 12, 36
    50, 51
high mass 19
his very looks 25
historically false .... xviii, 46
hit my opponents rather
    hard 14, 44
Hodges ...... x, 5, 6, 8, 9, 28, 55
Hodges & Farstad .... x, 9
Hodges and Farstad 6, 9, 55
Hodges-Farstad 5, 8
holy communion 18, 19
Holy Eucharist 19
Holy Ghost 13, 42, 50, 51
Holy Scripture xviii, 12, 43, 48, 51
Holy Scripture is inspired .. 12, 51
Holy Spirit of God 12, 36, 50
hope 14, 33, 44, 45
Hort 1, 5, 8, 9, 30-32
    35-37, 54, 55
How We Got Our Bible 24
ideologically true ...... xviii, 46
if executed with consummate
    ability 11
immoral characters .. xviii, 16, 46
imperilled words 30
In Defense of Traditional Bible
    Texts 40, 53, 54
incarnation 15, 45

incense 19
incredible folly .... ix, 3
indexed 7
indexing .... x, 7
indomitable force of will .. xiv, 25
inerrancy ... xi, xiii, xix, 1, 11, 13
    21, 27, 30, 33, 48
inerrant 27
inestimable value 11
infallible 27, 49
inferior version .... xvii, 39
infidel 15, 45, 48
infidelity .... xii, 16, 46
infinitely precious .... xv, 26
inspecting .... x, 7
inspiration ... xi, xiii, xv, xvi, xviii
    xix, 1, 11-17, 21, 23, 26, 28,
    32, 33, 35, 36, 42-52, 55
Inspiration and Interpretation ...
    12, 13, 15-17, 23, 32
    35, 36, 42,43, 45-52
inspired .... xi, xix, 12-14, 21, 32
    36, 44, 49-51, 55
inspired book ...... xi, xix, 13, 51
inspired entirely 12, 36, 50
inspired in every part .. xi, 13, 51
intrepidity 19, 26
intrinsic 9
intrinsic and transcriptional
    probabilities 9
Introductory Remarks ...... ix, 1
irreligion .... xii, 16, 46
Jack Moorman 4, 8, 9
Jewish history 15, 45
John William Burgon .. 1, 3, vii, 1
    10, 28, 52
join us 56
jot 26
judgment 15, 45
justification 15, 45
K.J.V. 1611 Compared to the
    Present 23
King James Bible x, xi, xiv, xvii, 5

62   Ten Reasons Why DBS Deserves Its Name

8, 10, 11, 20, 22, 24, 27,
28, 31, 35, 37, 39, 40, 43, 53, 55
languages .... x, 7, 12, 21, 22, 28
33, 36, 40, 49
Last Twelve Verses of Mark 23, 36
laughed at .... xv, 30, 31
Lectionaries .... x, 7-9
lectures 23
lesser details 4, 5
Letis, Theodore 10
letters ...... vii, xi, xix, 2, 11, 12
30, 33, 35, 36, 49-51
letters of it 12, 36, 50
liberal .... xi, xviii, 14, 31, 44, 45
liberal party .. xi, xviii, 14, 44, 45
lifelong familiarity 6
literal ..... xv, xvi, 27, 32-34, 40
literal and obvious sense 32
literary work .... xi, 10, 11
liturgies 15, 45
living Englishmen 6
looks 25
low mass 19
Majority Greek Text x, 5, 9, 10, 28
Majority Text 10, 43, 55
Majority Text Society 10, 43
marginal notes .... xi, 11
Mariolatry 19
Masoretic .... ix, xiii, xvii, 20-22
27, 28, 31, 37, 39, 40, 55
Masoretic Hebrew Text ...... ix,
xiii, xvii, 20-22, 27, 28
31, 37, 39, 40, 55
mass .... xii, 18, 19
Master .... ix, 3
mastered by Englishmen .... x, 7
materially erred 6
mature .... ix, 6
May 31, 1990 vii
men of 1611 .... x, 10
message book 24
Miller 4
miracles 15

misapprehension 13
Missing in Modern Bibles 4
misstatement 13, 51
misunderstanding ..... xvi, 36, 38
Moorman, Dr. Jack 4, 8, 9
motto .... xiii, 20, 53
NASV 37
Needed ...... vii, xx, 2, 14, 54-56
Neglected ... vii, xv, 2, 30, 31, 56
Nelson 6
neo-evangelical 27, 31
neo-evangelical compromises . 27
Nestle-Aland .... x, 5, 7, 8
Nestle-Aland 26th or 27th edition 5
Nestle-Aland Greek text ... x, 7, 8
never lead critical students . ix, 4, 5
New American Standard .. 24, 37
New International Version . 24, 37
New King James 23, 37
New Testament .... ix-xi, 1, 3, 4, 6
11, 20, 27, 30, 33, 35
39, 41, 42, 54, 55
New Testament Textus
  Receptus .... ix, 3
Newman 17
Newsletter 28
nine cases out of ten ...... ix, 4, 5
NIV 37
NKJV 37
no equal 21, 22, 27, 28, 40
no error or blot .... xi, 13, 51
no misapprehension or
  misstatement 13
no one will venture to predicate . 5
no revision 10
no revision of our Authorized
  Version 11
noblest literary work ... xi, 10, 11
not yet mature .... ix, 6
November 3-4, 1978 1
Obedient ... vii, xviii, xx, 2, 44, 47
52, 53, 56
obvious sense 32

Index of Words and Phrases 63

Old Testament ix, 3, 20, 27, 39, 40
once advanced 25
one issue 27, 40
one issue society 27, 40
opponents . . . . xi, 14, 44
Oriel College 18
original texts . . . 21, 22, 27, 28, 40
orthodoxy 6
outrageous manner . . . . xii, 16, 46
outspokenness 26
Oxford . . . . xi-xiii, xviii, 13-15, 17
18, 23, 44
Oxford Diocesan
 Conference . . . . xiii, 18
Oxford Movement 17
pamphlets . . . . xiv, 10, 23, 24
37, 43, 55
papyrus 8, 9
papyrus fragments 8, 9
perfection of God's Holy Word 18
Philadelphia 1
Philistines 10
Pickering 10
plenary . . . xi, xiii, xv, xvi, 11, 12
21, 32, 33
poison 46
prayer for the dead . . . . xii, 17
Prebendary Scrivener 6
precious . . viii, x, xv, 7, 26, 34, 40
precious blood of Christ 34
precious secrets . . . . x, 7
prerequisite #1 . . . . x, 6, 8, 9
prerequisite #2 . . . . x, 6, 8, 9
prerequisite #3 . . . . x, 7-9
prerequisite #4 . . . . x, 7-9
prerequisite #5 . . . . x, 7-9
prerequisite #6 . . . . x, 7-9
prerequisites . . . . . ix, x, 5, 6, 8-10
preserve the deposit 14, 44
preserved . . . 21, 22, 27, 28, 37, 40
preserved texts 21, 27
President, The Dean Burgon
 Society . . . . 1, 3, vii, 1

private edification . . . . xi, 11
probabilities 9
proficiency 6
proficiency in the best learning . . 6
profound theological learning . . 26
prophecy 15
prophets 16, 26, 46
Providentially preserved
 texts 21, 27
punctilious courtesy . . . xii, 16, 46
Pusey 17
quietest half-hour . . . . xix, 48
quite good enough . . . . ix, 4, 5
radio stations 31
ransacked 7
ransacking . . . . x, 7
rationalism . . . . . xii, 14, 18, 26, 44
read every book 48
read the whole Bible
 consecutively 48
reading an inspired book xi, 13, 51
recall their words . . . . . . xii, 17, 47
Received Greek Text . xvii, 21, 22,
27, 28, 31, 37, 39-41, 55
Received Text . . . . ix, 5, 22
received text is the true one 5
redeeming blood 27, 34
redemption 15, 45
reference 11
regeneration 15
Relevant . . . vii, xvii, 2, 39, 40, 56
reprobation . . . . xviii, 17, 47
requires revision 5
resign . . . . xii, xviii, 17, 47
resign their stations . . . . . xii, xviii
17, 47
resurrection . . . . xii, 15, 16, 24
40, 45, 47
Revelation . . . . xv, 9, 21, 32
33, 42, 49, 55
revelation from God 55
reverence for the Word of God . 26
Reviewer 15, 45, 46

revised edition 11
Revised Version . . xiii, xv, xvi, 19
    20, 22, 30, 35, 37, 39
revising 6
revising the sacred text 6
revision . . . . ix-xi, xiii, 4-8, 10, 11
    14, 19, 20, 23, 30
    35-37, 39
revision of the Textus Receptus ix,
    x, 5, 6, 8, 10
Revision Revised . . . 5-7, 10, 11, 14
    19, 20, 23, 35-37, 39, 44
revolutionising 14
revolutionising Oxford 14
ridicule . . . . xviii, 17, 47
ritual . . . . xii, 18
ritualists . . . . xiii, 19
rival translation . . . . xi, 11
Roman mass . . . . xii, 18
Romanism . . . . xii, xiii, 17, 21
Romanism I abhor 17
romanizing . . . . xii, 17, 18
romanizing tendencies 17
Romish doctrines . . . . xiii, 19
Ruckman, Dr. Peter 55
run with it 52
sacred text . . . . xiii, 6, 20
Sacred Trust 15
Saint worship 19
salvation . . . . xvi, 2, 15, 24, 33, 40
scholarlike . . . . x, 7
scholarlike manner . . . . x, 7
scholarship 1, 6
science of textual criticism . x, 6, 7
Scrivener, Dr. Frederick 6, 30
season 14, 44
Second Person 15, 45
secrets . . . . x, 7
sentences of it 12, 36, 50, 51
separation 14, 24, 27, 40
seriously astray . . . . ix, 4, 5
seriously imperilled . . . . . xi, xviii
    14, 44

sermons . . . . xii, 18
Seven Defects 10
Sinai 54
sincerity . . . . xiv, 25
six . . . . . ix-xiii, xv, xvi, xviii, 5, 6
    8-11, 15, 16, 21, 27
    32-34, 40, 45, 46,
six clergymen . xviii, 15, 16, 45, 46
six literal solar days 27, 34
six of its authors 15, 45
six ordinary days 32
six prerequisites . . . . ix, x, 6, 8-10
sixty-six canonical books . . 21, 33
smallest danger . . . . . xi, 13, 14, 44
softened 17, 47
solar days 27, 34
speaking sharply 14, 44
species of treason 16, 46
Spirit of their God . . . . x, 10
splendid scholarship 6
spurious Greek text 30
stick to our colours 25
stood and acted alone 25
strong hearts 25
strong unwavering hand 52
study . . . . xi, xvi, xix, 3, 10, 11, 19
    21, 27, 28, 36, 37, 39
    42, 43, 48, 51, 52
substance 13, 19, 51
supreme 13, 50, 51
surrenders the first page 50
sweet tempers 25
Sword of the Lord 31, 43
syllable . . . . xi, 12, 36, 49, 50
syllables 11, 12, 35, 36, 49-51
syllables of it 12, 36, 50
Table of Contents ix
TBS 10
TBS in London 10
ten or twenty years 6
Ten Reasons . . . . vii, 2
Ten Reasons Why the DBS
    Deserves its Name 2

Index of Words and Phrases

tenacity of purpose 25
Terence Brown 10
Textual Commentary on Matthew 4
textual criticism . . . . . x, 1, 6-9, 30
Textus Receptus . . . ix, x, xiii, 3-6
          8-10, 20, 31
Textus Receptus Greek Text . ix, 3
Textus Receptus revision 4, 5
The Traditional Text . . . . . xiii, 23
          30, 36, 39
theistic 34
Theodore Letis 10
time for speaking sharply . . 14, 44
tinkering . . . . ix, 3, 39
tinkering the Hebrew text ix, 3, 39
tittle 26
too hard 14, 44
too straight 14, 44
torch of truth 52
tracts 24, 37
Traditional Greek Text 20, 23
          27, 54
Traditional Text . . . . . xiii, 23, 30
          36, 39, 54
trained Greek scholar 54
transcriptional 9
transfiguration 46
translation . . . xi, 11, 20-22, 27, 28
       33, 35, 37, 40, 49, 55
transubstantiation 19
treason 16, 46
treasured 26
Trinitarian Bible Society . . . 10, 20
          21, 41, 43
true one 5
trumpet 25
trumpet gave no uncertain
 sound 25
Tyndale 10
unanimous 6
uncertain sound 25
uncials 8, 9

uncompromising 26
Undaunted . . . vii, xvi, 2, 35-38, 56
underlying original texts 22, 28, 40
undermining the faith . . . . . xii, 18
undivided attention 6
unequally inspired 13, 51
unerring 13, 50, 51
unflinching conservatism xii
           14, 45
university . . . xi, 13-15, 19, 23, 45
University of Oxford 15
unlimited inerrancy 27
unpublished works . . . . x, 7
unqualified reprobation . . . .
         xviii, 17, 47
untrustworthy . . . . xiii, 20
unwavering hand 52
unyieldedness 25
utterance of the Eternal . 12, 36, 50
value 11
variety of sources 5
Vatican 54
verbal . . . . . xi, xiii, xv, xvi, xix, 1
     11, 12, 21, 32, 33, 36, 49
verbal inspiration . xi, xiii, xv, xvi
       xix, 1, 11, 12, 21
        32, 33, 36, 49
verses 11, 12, 21, 23, 27
        33, 35, 36, 49
versions . . x, xvi, xvii, 7-10, 37, 40
very letters . . . . xi, 12, 36, 50
very utterance of the Holy
 Ghost 13, 51
vestments 19
Vicar of St. Mary the Virgin's . 18
vicarious death 34
video . . . . vii, xiv, 24, 55
video cassettes . . . . xiv, 24, 55
Waite . . . . 1, 3, vi, vii, 1
Warren, Maine vii
watchful 52
watch-dog . . . . xi, 13, 14, 44
weapon . . . . xx, 52

Westcott ... xiii, xvi, 1, 5, 8, 9, 21
    22, 30-32, 35-37, 54, 55
Westcott and Hort .. 1, 8, 9, 30-32
    35, 37, 54, 55
Westcott-Hort 5
Westcott-Hort Greek text 5
when unanimous 6
Wilbur Pickering 10
William Tyndale 10
Word of God   xiv, xv, xviii, 13, 15
    21, 23, 26, 27, 30, 32
    33, 42, 43, 45, 49-51, 53
words .. xi, xii, xvi, xviii, xix, 2, 4
    11-14, 17, 21, 25, 27, 30, 35-
    37, 42, 44, 47, 49-51, 57
words of inspiration .. xi, xviii, 14
    44
words of it 12, 13, 36, 50, 51
words of that text to be
    inspired 13, 51
words of the Bible to be
    inspired 12, 36, 49
work of real genius .... x, 10
written in his very looks 25
written ministry ...... xvi, 36, 37
Zane Hodges 28

About the Author

The author of this book, Dr. D. A. Waite, received a B.A. (Bachelor of Arts) in classical Greek and Latin from the University of Michigan in 1948, a Th.M. (Master of Theology), with high honors, in New Testament Greek Literature and Exegesis from Dallas Theological Seminary in 1952, an M.A. (Master of Arts) in Speech from Southern Methodist University in 1953, a Th.D. (Doctor of Theology), with honors, in Bible Exposition from Dallas Theological Seminary in 1955, and a Ph.D. in Speech from Purdue University in 1961. He holds both New Jersey and Pennsylvania teacher certificates in Greek and Language Arts.

He has been a teacher in the areas of Greek, Hebrew, Bible, Speech, and English for over thirty-five years in nine schools, including one junior high, one senior high, three Bible institutes, two colleges, two universities, and one seminary. He served his country as a Navy Chaplain for five years on active duty; pastored three churches; was Chairman and Director of the Radio and Audio-Film Commission of the American Council of Christian Churches; since 1971, has been Founder, President, and Director of THE BIBLE FOR TODAY; since 1978, has been President of the DEAN BURGON SOCIETY; since 1998, has been Pastor of THE BIBLE FOR TODAY BAPTIST CHURCH with his sermons and other messages heard daily all over the world on www.Bible ForToday. org by means of the internet; has produced over 900 other studies, books, cassettes, or VCR's on various topics; and is heard on both a five-minute daily and thirty-minute weekly radio program IN DEFENSE OF TRADITIONAL BIBLE TEXTS. Dr. and Mrs. Waite have been married since 1948; they have four sons, one daughter, and, at present, eight grandchildren.

Order Blank (p. 1)

Name:_____

Address:_____

City & State:_____Zip:_____

Credit Card #:_____Expires:_____

[ ] (#1847) *10 Reasons Why DBS Deserves its Name* by DAW ($6+$3 S&H ask for quantity prices)

[ ] *Inspiration and Interpretation* (#1220) by Dean Burgon ($25+$5 S&H) A hardback book, 523 pages in length.
[ ] *The Last 12 Verses of Mark* (#1139) by Dean Burgon ($15+$5) perfect-bound book 400 pages in length.
[ ] *The Revision Revised* (#611) by Dean Burgon ($25+$5) A hardback book, 640 pages in length.
[ ] *The Traditional Text* (#611) hardback by Burgon ($16+$5) A hardback book, 384 pages in length.
[ ] *Causes of Corruption* (#1159) hardback by Burgon ($15+$4) A hardback book, 360 pages in length.
[ ] Send <u>all five</u> of Dean Burgon's books (*Last 12 verses, Revision Revised, Traditional Text, Causes of Corruption, & Inspiration and Interpretation*). ($96 value for $75+S&H)

[ ] (#2506) DAW's Summary defending *Mark 16:9-20* ($3+$3)
[ ] (#2695) *Westcott & Hort's Greek Text & Theory Refuted by Burgon's Revision Revised--Summarized* by Dr. D. A. Waite ($4.00 + $3 S&H)
[ ] (#2771) *Summary of Traditional Text* by Dr. Waite ($3+$2)
[ ] (#2780) *Summary of Causes of Corruption*, DAW ($3+$2)
[ ] (#2925) *Summary of Inspiration and Interpretation* by Dr. Waite ($4 + $2)

Send or Call Orders to:
THE DEAN BURGON SOCIETY
Box 354, Collingswood, NJ 08108
Phone: 856-854-4452; FAX:--2464; Orders: 1-800 JOHN 10:9
E-Mail: DBS@DeanBurgonSociety.org; Credit Cards OK
Order all materials Online: www.BibleForToday.org

Order Blank (p. 2)

Name:_____

Address:_____

City & State:_____ Zip:_____

Credit Card #:_____ Expires:_____

Other Materials on the KJB & T.R.
[ ] *Defending the King James Bible* (#1594-P) by Dr.Waite ($12+$4) A hardback book, indexed with study questions.
[ ] *The Case for the King James Bible* (#83) by DAW ($7+ $4 S&H) A perfect bound book, 112 pages in length.
[ ] *Foes of the King James Bible Refuted* (#2777) by DAW ($9 +$4 S&H) A perfect bound book, 164 pages in length.
[ ] *Burgon's Warnings on Revision* (#804) by DAW ($7+$3 S&H) A perfect bound book, 120 pages in length.
[ ] (#1131) *Westcott's Denial of Resurrection*, by DAW ($4+$3)
[ ] (#2423) *Four Reasons for Defending KJB* by DAW ($2+$3)

[ ] (#2928) *Fundamentalist Distortions on Bible Versions* by Dr. D. A. Waite ($7+$3 S&H) (7 Schools Refuted)
[ ] (#2974) *Fundamentalist MIS-INFORMATION on Bible Versions* by Dr. D. A. Waite ($7+$3 S&H) (*Mind of Man*)

[ ] (#2721) *Contemporary Eng. Version Exposed*, DAW-$3+$2
[ ] (#743) *Guide to Textual Criticism* by Edward Miller ($7+$4)
[ ] (#2591) *Dean Burgon's Confidence in KJB* DAW ($3+$3)
[ ] (#2671) *Readability of A.V. (KJB)* D.A.waite, Jr. ($5 +$3)
[ ] (#2768) *NIV Inclusive Language Exposed* by DAW ($4+$3)
[ ] Send *26 Hours of KJB Seminar* (4 videos) by DAW ($50.00)
[ ] (#3000L) *Defined King James Bible* lg.prt. leath.-$40+S&H
[ ] (#958) The "DBS Articles of Faith & Organization" (N.C.)
[ ] Brochure #1: "1000 Titles Defending KJB/TR"(N.C.)

Send or Call Orders to:
THE DEAN BURGON SOCIETY
Box 354, Collingswood, NJ 08108
Phone: 856-854-4452; FAX:--2464; Orders: 1-800 JOHN 10:9
E-Mail: DBS@DeanBurgonSociety.org; Credit Cards OK
Order all materials Online: www.BibleForToday.org

Order Blank (p. 3)

Name:_____

Address:_____

City & State:_____ Zip:_____

Credit Card #:_____ Expires:_____

More Materials on the KJB &T.R.

[ ] *Heresies of Westcott & Hort* (#595) by Dr. Waite ($4+$3)

[ ] *Scrtvener's Greek New Testament Underlying the King James Bible*, (#471) hardback, ($14+$5 S&H*)*

[ ] *Scrivener's Annotated Greek New Testament with Westcott & Changes to the Textus Receptus* (#1670), 667 pp., hardback ($35+$5 S&H); leather ($45+$5 S&H).

[ ] (#2562) *Why Not the King James Bible?--Answer to James White's KJVO Book* by Dr. K. D. DiVietro, ($9+$5 S&H)

[ ] (#1428) *Forever Settled--Bible Documents & History Survey* by Dr. Jack Moorman, ($20+$5 S&H)

[ ] (#2136) *Early Church Fathers & the A.V.--A Demonstration* by Dr. Jack Moorman, ($6 + $4 S&H).

[ ] (#1617) *When the KJB Departs from the So-Called "Majority Text"* by Dr. Jack Moorman, ($16 + $4 S&H)

[ ] (#1726) *Missing in Modern Bibles--Nestle-Aland & NIV Errors* by Dr. Jack Moorman, ($8 + $4 S&H)

[ ] (#2726VCR) *The Doctrinal Heart of the Bible--Removed from Modern Versions* by Dr. Jack Moorman, ($15 +$5)

[ ] (#2623) *Modern Bibles--The Dark Secret* by Dr. Jack Moorman, ($3+$2 S&H)

[ ] (#1825) *Early Manuscripts and the A.V.--A Closer Look,* by Dr. Jack Moorman, ($15+$4 S&H)

Send or Call Orders to:
THE DEAN BURGON SOCIETY
Box 354, Collingswood, NJ 08108
Phone: 856-854-4452; FAX:--2464; Orders: 1-800 JOHN 10:9
E-Mail: DBS@DeanBurgonSociety.org; Credit Cards OK
Order all materials Online: www.BibleForToday.org

The Defined King James Bible

WITH UNCOMMON WORDS DEFINED

I. Deluxe Genuine Leather

✦Large Print--Black or Burgundy✦
1 for $40.00+S&H
✦Case of 12 for✦
$30.00 each+S&H

✦Medium Print--Black or Burgundy✦
1 for $35.00+S&H
✦Case of 12 for✦
$25.00 each+S&H

II. Deluxe Hardbacks

Large: 1 for $20.00+S&H;
Case of 12 for $15 each+S&H

Medium: 1 for $15.00+S&H
Case of 12 for $10 each+S&H

Order Phone: 1-800-JOHN 10:9

CREDIT CARDS WELCOMED

Send Gift Subscriptions
All gifts to Dean Burgon Society are tax deductible!

THE DEAN BURGON SOCIETY
Box 354 - Collingswood, New Jersey 08108, U.S.A.,
Phone; (856) 854-4452; FAX: (856) 854-2464

Membership Form

I have a copy of the "**Articles of faith. Operation and Organization**" of The Dean Burgon Society, Incorporated. After reading these "Articles," I wish to state, by my signature below, that I believe in and accept such "Articles." I understand that my "Membership" is for one year and that I must renew my "Membership" at that time in order to remain a "Member" in good standing 6f the Society.

[ ] I wish to become a member of The Dean Burgon Society for the first time.
[ ] I wish to renew my membership subscription which has expired as of:_____
SIGNED:_____
DATE:_____
I enclose: **Attention: The Dean Burgon Society**
    Box 354 - Collingswood, Now Jersey 08108
*Membership Donation: ($7.00/year) $_____
*Life Membership Donation: ($50.00) $_____
*Additional Donation To The Society: $_____
        TOTAL: $_____
Please PRINT In CAPITAL LETTERS your name and address below:
NAME:_____
ADDRESS:_____
CITY:_____
STATE:_____ ZIP:_____

  Although I am not a member of **The Dean Burgon Society**, I do wish to subscribe to the **Newsletter,** by making a gift of **$3.50** to the Society.
NAME:_____
ADDRESS:_____
CITY:_____
STATE:_____ ZIP:_____
*1 understand that, included in my **first $3.50 gift** accompanying any donation or order regardless of the amount of the order or donation, is my year's subscription to **The Dean Burgon Society NEWSLETTER.**
    Canada & All Foreign Subscriptions $7.00 Yearly

www.ingramcontent.com/pod-product-compliance
Lightning Source LLC
Chambersburg PA
CBHW060401050426
42449CB00009B/1850